No. 31

64 PAGES OF Thrill-Packed ACTION

SEPTEMBER, 1939

Detective COMICS

Reg. U. S. Pat. Office

10¢

Powerful and awesome, the mysterious BATMAN again appears to oppose the evil forces of a terrifying master of crime known as THE MONK!

THE GOLDEN AGE OF

BAT MAN ®

THE GREATEST COVERS OF

Detective COMICS ®

FROM THE '30s TO THE '50s

ARTABRAS

NEW YORK · LONDON · PARIS

TEXT: **Joe Desris**
EDITORS: **Amy Handy (Abbeville); Charles Kochman, Steven Korté (DC Comics)**
PRODUCTION EDITOR: **Owen Dugan**
PRODUCTION SUPERVISOR: **Simone René**

First edition

Many of the covers reproduced in this volume were provided from the private collections of Craig Delich, Joe Desris, Ron Killian, and Mike Tiefenbacher. All cover credits researched and assembled by Joe Desris.

The captions note the pencil and ink artists for each cover as could best be determined; however, as it was not standard practice to credit artists in the comic-book industry until the last few decades, this list may not be definitive. While the authors have endeavored to identify all of the artists involved, they apologize to any person misidentified or not identified and invite such person to inform them of the error.

Library of Congress Cataloging-in-Publication Data

The Golden age of Batman : the greatest covers of Detective comics from the '30s to the '50s
      p.   cm.
    Introd. by Joe Desris.
    Includes index.
    ISBN 0-89660-046-7
    I. Batman (Comic strip)   2. Comic book covers—United States.
I. Desris, Joe.   II. Batman (Comic strip)   III. Detective comics.
PN6728.B36G65   1994
741.5'973—dc20   **93-42383**

Contents

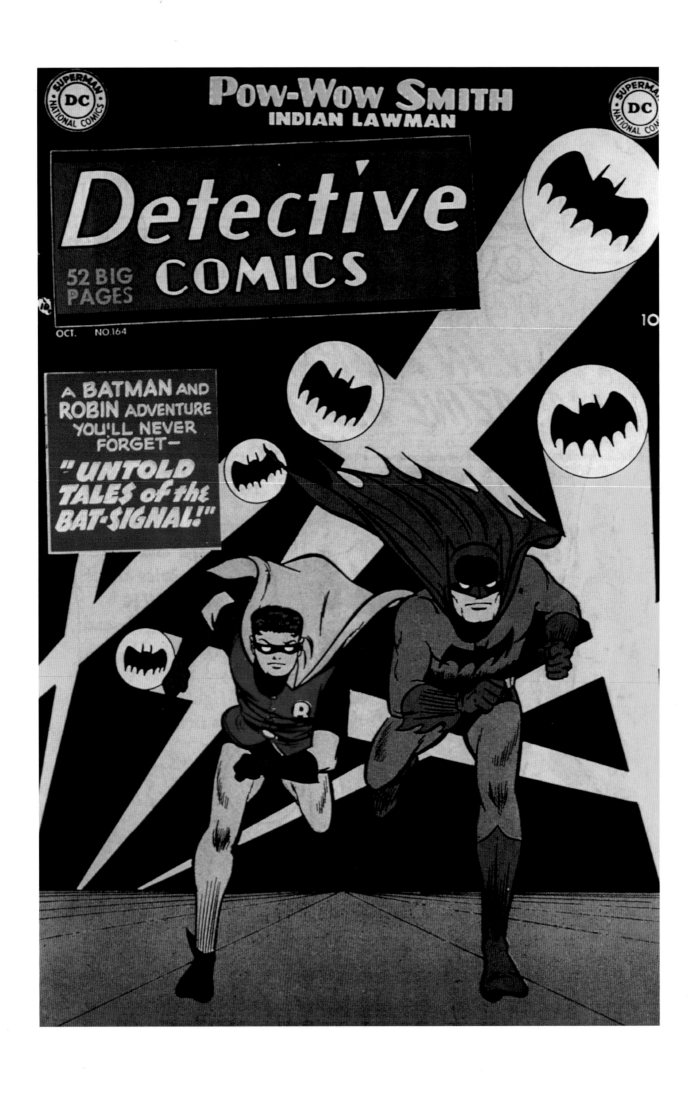

Introduction

By Joe Desris

"What is a Bat-Man?" asked DC Comics publisher Jack Liebowitz.

"He's a crime fighter who wears a bat costume," replied cartoonist Bob Kane.

"It looks kind of mysterious and creepy," responded Liebowitz. "Do you think the public will like it?"

Such is the conversation Kane recalls upon presenting his initial Batman sketches at the offices of DC Comics in 1938. Just a few months later, Batman's first adventure, "The Case of the Chemical Syndicate," appeared in *Detective Comics* issue 27 (May 1939). Superman's success in 1938 had paved the way for the costumed-hero comic, but Kane fortunately did not encounter the lengthy delays and difficulties in finding a publisher that had plagued Superman's creators, Jerry Siegel and Joe Shuster.

Batman was indeed a creation of Kane—with, as he admits, a little help from popular culture such as Zorro, movies, and pulp magazines. But the final version of the Dark Knight that appeared in print was actually a collaborative effort between Kane and writer Bill Finger. It was Finger who suggested giving Batman a cowl and gauntlets, replacing his eyes with white slits, and changing his costume from red to dark gray. He also wrote Batman's first two adventures and later chronicled some of the most memorable villains, plots, and sets, including giant clock towers, oversized typewriters, and seemingly inescapable doom traps.

With Batman's incredible worldwide success nowadays, it is hard to believe he was ever less than familiar. Yet the Dark Knight took a little longer than his Kryptonian counterpart to reach icon status— about twenty-five years. This is not to say that Batman was not a hot property from the beginning. After only eight appearances, Batman usurped the regular cover position with *Detective Comics* issue 35. In addition to those monthly adventures, he earned his own comic-book title in 1940, began appearing in *World's Finest Comics* in 1941, had his own newspaper strip in 1943, and made it to the silver screen with a fifteen-chapter serial, also in 1943. But it took the 1966–68 "Batman" TV series to make Batman a household name. And it was Frank Miller's *Batman: The Dark Knight*, a 1986 four-part graphic novel, along with the astoundingly successful 1989 feature film *Batman*, that etched the Gotham Guardian's name and image into public consciousness. Several years ago, a syndicated gag-panel newspaper strip depicted a TV news crew in the front yard of the only man in America without a Batman T-shirt.

Serious Batman merchandising developed due to the popularity of the '60s TV series. With Batman bread, peanut butter and jelly, bubble-gum cards, bolo ties, puzzles, metal lunch boxes, model kits, and wallpaper (to name just a few), the Caped Crusader seemed to be turning up everywhere. Although the Ajax Toy Co.'s Batplanes and Batmobiles on cover 197 (see page 110) would seem to imply the existence of such items in 1953, few Batman toys were licensed at that point.

Surely much of Batman's appeal stems from the fact that he is a regular guy. He is an unusually well-disciplined human being, but still he is human, even if he is a millionaire socialite in his street clothes. Batman is not from another planet, was not bitten by a radioactive spider, and does not have to utter mysterious incantations or swallow special potions to morph into a crime fighter. He simply puts on his uniform and goes to work, just like a member of the police force. He does not possess traditional superpowers like X-ray vision or the ability to fly. Nevertheless, his vast knowledge, resources, and finely honed skills parallel such powers, making the Gotham Guardian a mortal yet highly determined and virtually unconquerable opponent.

According to the comic-book chronicles, a very young Bruce Wayne experienced the trauma of seeing his parents murdered. The orphaned Wayne developed his crime-fighting abilities over a fifteen-year period, becoming adept at acrobatics, boxing, science, and detective skills. When a bat flew into the Wayne Manor study one evening, Wayne found the omen he needed to embark on his crime-fighting career. Combined with a strong sense of honesty and justice, the Masked Manhunter became an obsessed, relentless, and potentially lethal fighting machine (though he is bound by his own personal code that forbids killing). An unequaled tactician and strategist, he is also an expert at disguises and a master of nearly all forms of physical combat. At his disposal is a vast array of high-tech equipment and weaponry, including the Batmobile, Batplane, Batboat, Batcycle, and Batarang. His utility belt contains such devices as a laser torch, a miniature camera, skeleton keys, explosives, acids, tear-gas pellets, and a two-way radio.

Batman fought crime solo for eleven adventures before Robin was introduced. Young Dick Grayson—whose parents were also murdered—became Robin, the Boy Wonder. Alongside Batman, he brought his parents' assailants to justice. Wayne also obtained guardianship of Grayson (since Wayne was a bachelor he could not adopt him). Although the words "Batman and Robin" now seem as inseparable as "macaroni and cheese," the name Robin was chosen after some effort. Writer Bill Finger's original list included such monikers as Socko, Tiger, and Wildcat, and in fact the name Robin supposedly was not even on that first list.

While *Detective Comics* would eventually become an exclusive vehicle for Batman, the title began as a mystery/detective anthology with brand-new stories. Since many early comics had simply carried reprints, new material was still a comparative novelty in 1937 when the series began. The gun-toting cops and robbers of those pre-Batman issues offered a hint of the detective story content, although such covers were designed more to sell comics than highlight any particular story. Contents included Fred Guardineer's Speed Saunders, Jerry Siegel and Joe Shuster's Spy and Slam Bradley, as well as later appearances by Jim Chambers' Crimson Avenger and others such as Cosmo, Buck Marshall, Larry Steele and Dr. Fu Manchu. Most of these characters were featured on early covers at some point. Even Bob Kane's humor sub-

missions (Oscar the Gumshoe, Spanky and Cranky, Jest A Second) appeared inside *Detective Comics* before a successful Caped Crusader completely consumed Kane's time. As Batman's popularity demanded more material, it became increasingly difficult for one individual to maintain the pace. From late 1943 until late 1946, Kane essentially stopped pencilling comic-book stories and covers to work on the syndicated Batman newspaper strip.

As the chapters in this volume indicate, common themes and interpretations can be found throughout the covers. These images depict numerous successful bat-concepts such as the Batcave, the Bat-Signal, the Batmobile, the utility belt, and of course the incredible villains. While the characters and settings are malleable, resilient, and capable of enduring updates, they are in many respects inviolable. Perhaps it is an ability to change while retaining familiarity that makes Batman's world so memorable. The body of work stands as a monument to Bill Finger and Bob Kane. There will always be a Batman, and these men made him right the first time.

MARCH 1937; NO. 1
Cover artist: Vincent Sullivan

Cops, Crooks, and Creeps

As its title suggests, an exciting array of mystery stories awaited eager readers of *Detective Comics*. Good guys like Speed Saunders, Larry Steele, Slam Bradley, and Spy chased a series of nefarious felons, all of whom were obviously up to no good, and several of whom must surely have made the FBI's ten most ugly list. The daring detectives not only pursued the criminal and underworld elements, but caught them as well—in the nick of time and in exciting pulp fashion, as demonstrated on covers 5, 9, 28, and 32.

Gotham City's most famous detective ultimately usurped the coveted cover position with issue 35. But long after Batman had clearly become the title's main attraction, the book still continued the adventures of other sleuths, including Pow-Wow Smith, Indian Lawman; Captain Compass; and Roy Raymond, TV Detective. It was not until the 1980s that *Detective Comics* became completely dominated by the Gotham Guardian, as he finally took control of all interior story pages as well.

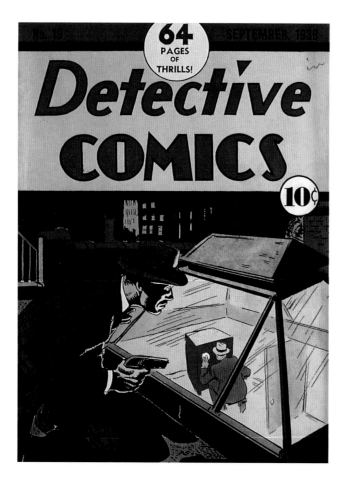

SEPTEMBER 1938; NO. 19
Cover artist: Creig Flessel

MARCH 1939; NO. 25
Cover artist: Fred Guardineer

NOVEMBER 1938; NO. 21
Cover artist: Leo E. O'Mealia

JUNE 1937; NO. 4
Cover artist: Creig Flessel

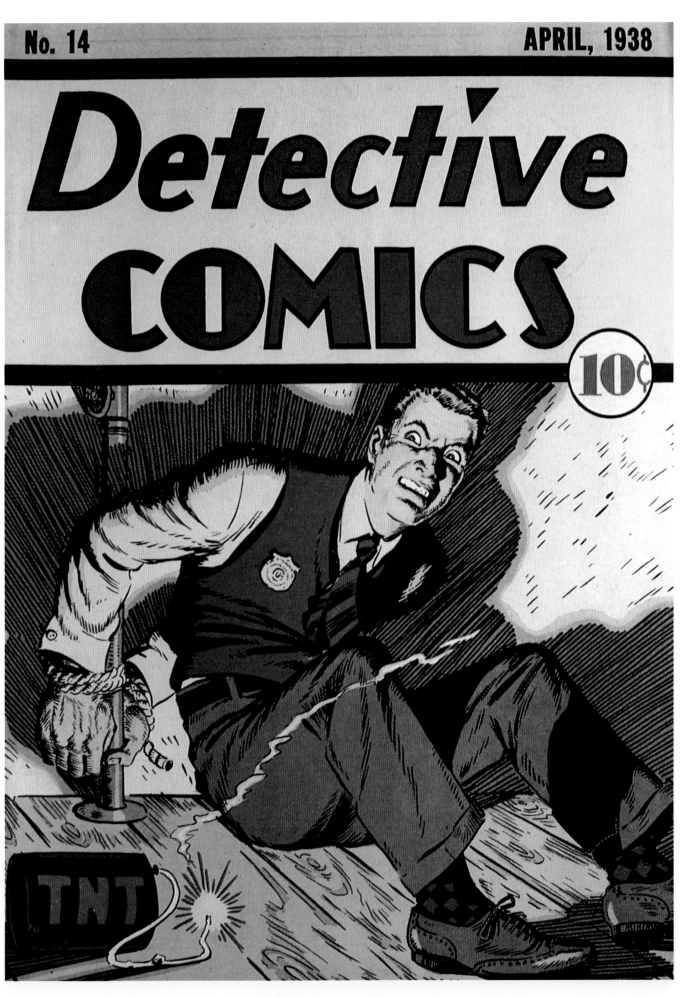

APRIL 1938; NO. 14
Cover artist: Creig Flessel

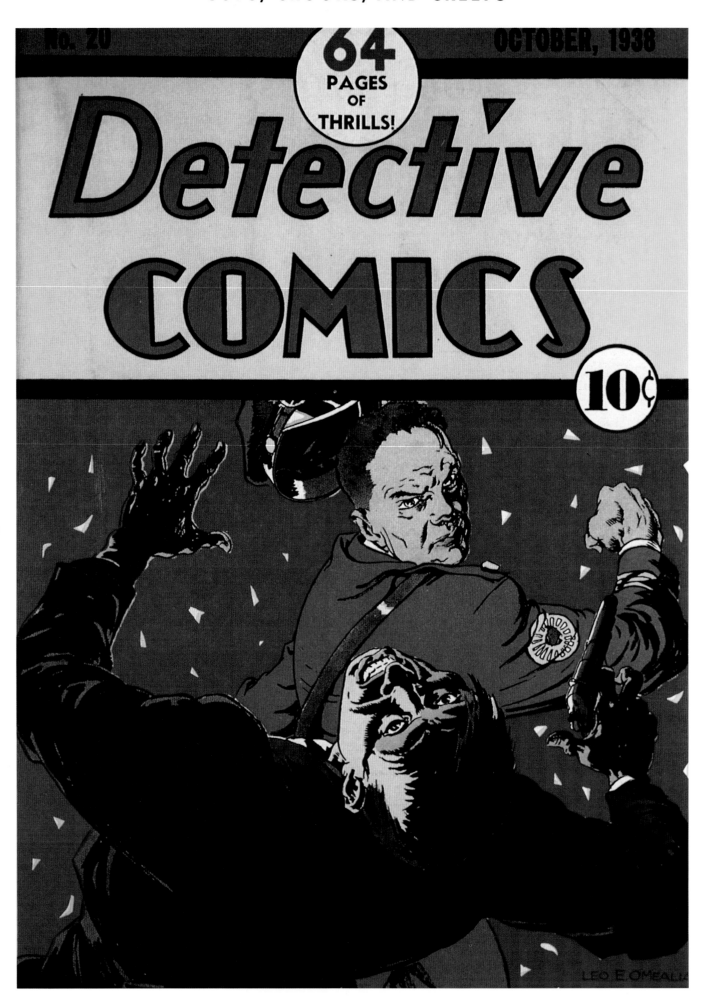

OCTOBER 1938; NO. 20
Cover artist: Leo E. O'Mealia

JULY 1937; NO. 5
Cover artist: Creig Flessel

DECEMBER 1937; NO. 10
Cover artist: Creig Flessel

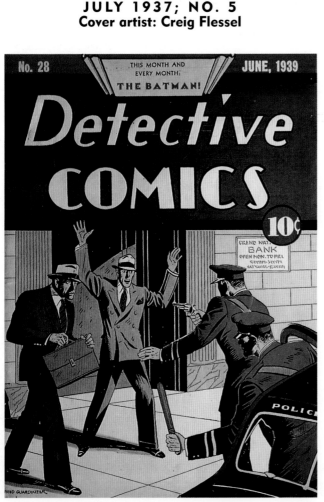

JUNE 1939; NO. 28
Cover artist: Fred Guardineer

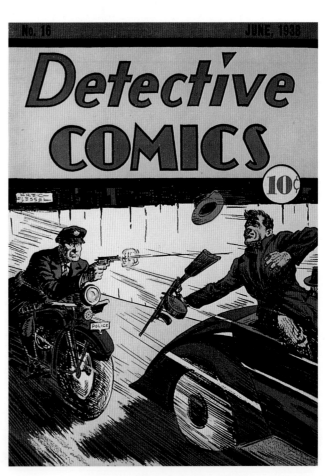

JUNE 1938; NO. 16
Cover artist: Creig Flessel

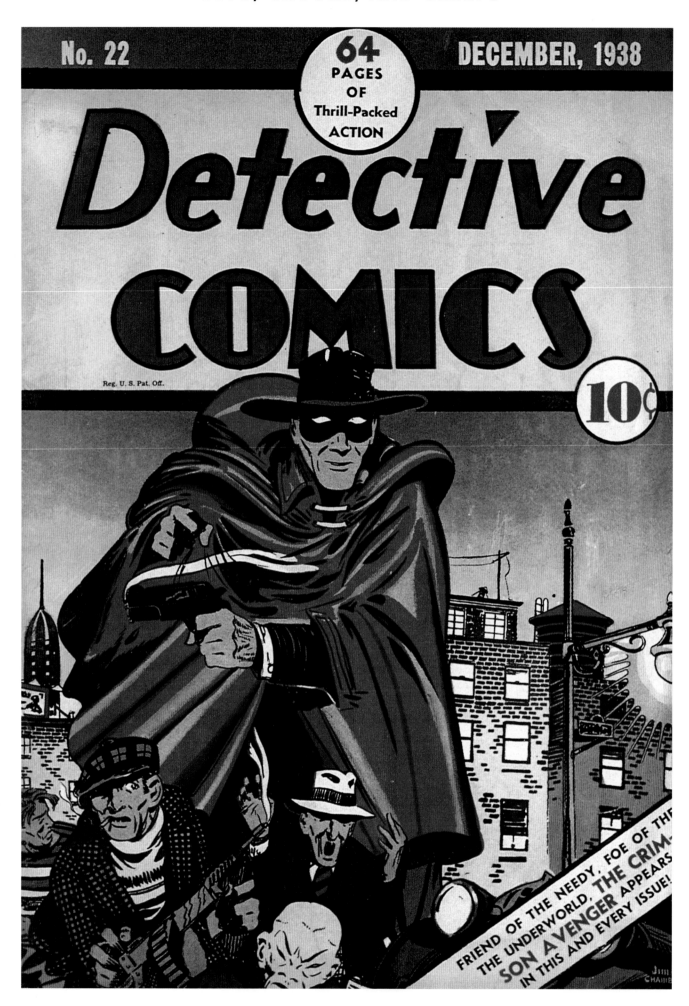

DECEMBER 1938; NO. 22
Cover artist: Jim Chambers

NOVEMBER 1937; NO. 9
Cover artist: Creig Flessel

FEBRUARY 1938; NO. 12
Cover artist: Creig Flessel

OCTOBER 1939; NO. 32
Cover artist: Fred Guardineer

SEPTEMBER 1937; NO. 7
Cover artist: Creig Flessel

MAY 1938; NO. 15
Cover artist: Creig Flessel

JANUARY 1939; NO. 23
Cover artist: Fred Guardineer

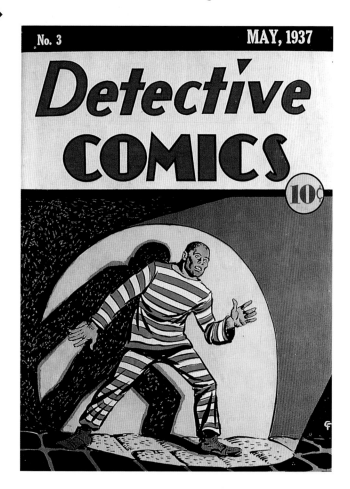

MAY 1937; NO. 3
Cover artist: Creig Flessel

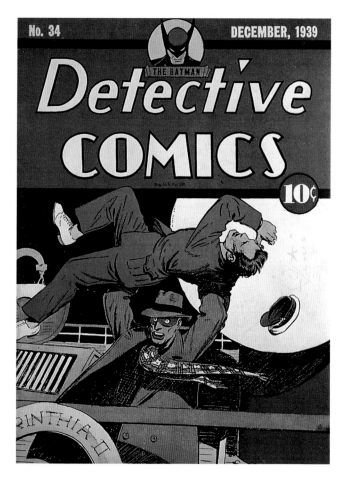

DECEMBER 1939; NO. 34
Cover artist: Creig Flessel

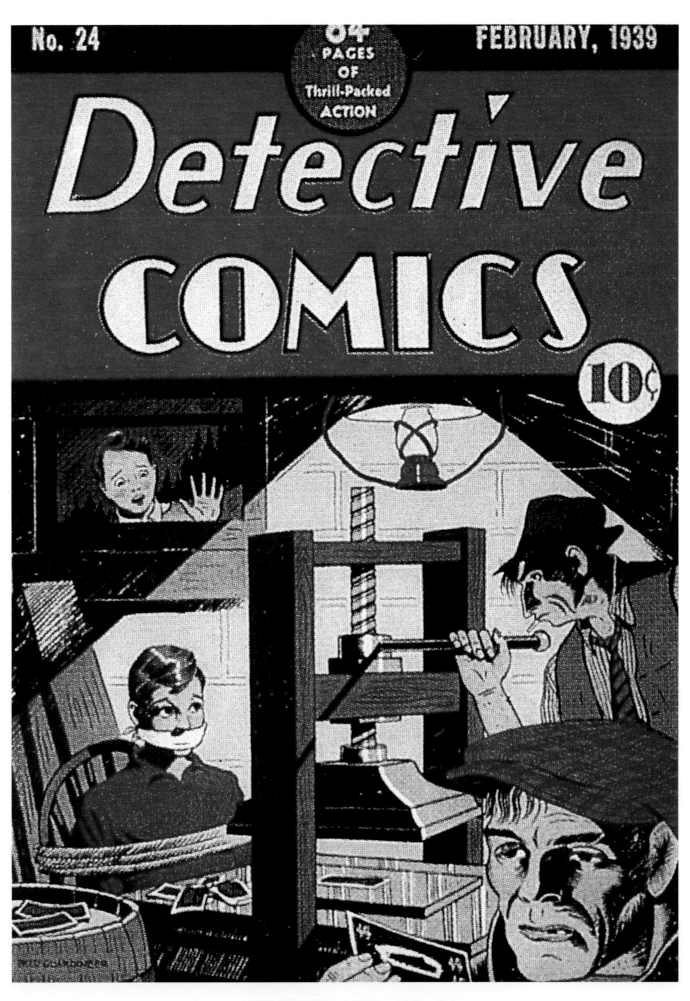

FEBRUARY 1939; NO. 24
Cover artist: Fred Guardineer

APRIL 1937; NO. 2
Cover artist: Creig Flessel

MARCH 1938; NO. 13
Cover artist: Creig Flessel

AUGUST 1937; NO. 6
Cover artist: Creig Flessel

APRIL 1939; NO. 26
Cover artist: Fred Guardineer

JULY 1938; NO. 17
Cover artist: Creig Flessel

AUGUST 1939; NO. 30
Cover artist: Fred Guardineer

JANUARY 1938; NO. 11
Cover artist: Creig Flessel

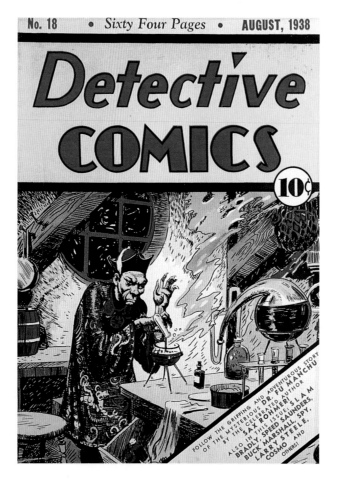

AUGUST 1938; NO. 18
Cover artist: Creig Flessel

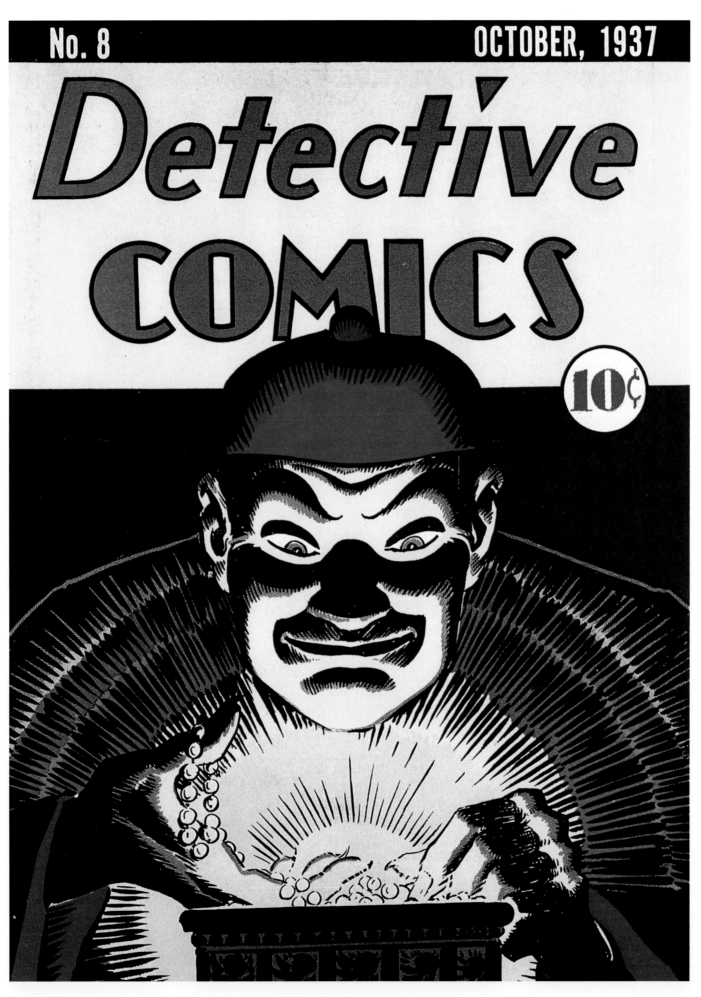

No. 8   OCTOBER, 1937

Detective COMICS

10¢

OCTOBER 1937; NO. 8
Cover artist: Creig Flessel

MAY 1939; NO. 27
Cover artist: Bob Kane

Caped Crusader

Batman's first adventure appeared in *Detective Comics* number 27. Throughout the earliest stories, he was portrayed as a powerful, awesome, and mysterious opponent of evil, a shadowy avenger who often worked in darkness and alone. (Robin was not introduced until a year later.)

Monstrously large capes in the early days heightened the Dark Knight's surrealism. In his earliest incarnations Batman is endowed with wings akin to an actual bat, but his attire was soon rendered in more traditional super-hero fashion. A more fluid cape added grandeur, motion, and drama, so it was broadened, lengthened, or otherwise redesigned for theatrical purposes as the cover artists saw fit. Superseding real-world considerations of wind direction, fabric weight, or maneuverability, the capes at times appear positively possessed. It seems to have been surprisingly windy when Batman and Robin arrived at the scene of a crime, as if the capes had minds of their own.

AUGUST 1941; NO. 54
Cover artists: Bob Kane, Jerry Robinson,
George Roussos

NOVEMBER 1939; NO. 33
Cover artist: Bob Kane

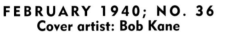

FEBRUARY 1940; NO. 36
Cover artist: Bob Kane

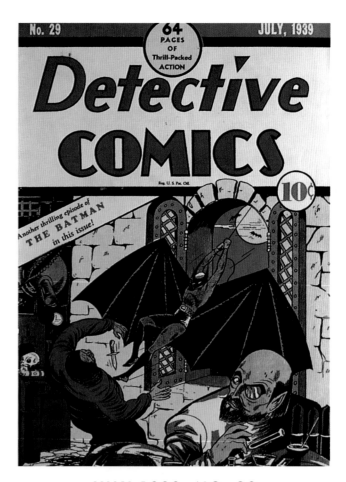

JULY 1939; NO. 29
Cover artist: Bob Kane

JULY 1940; NO. 41
Cover artists: Bob Kane, Jerry Robinson

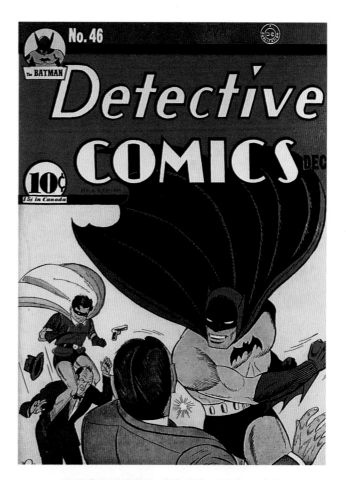

FEBRUARY 1941; NO. 48
Cover artists: Bob Kane, Jerry Robinson,
George Roussos

DECEMBER 1940; NO. 46
Cover artists: Bob Kane, Jerry Robinson,
George Roussos

OCTOBER 1940; NO. 44
Cover artists: Bob Kane, Jerry Robinson,
George Roussos

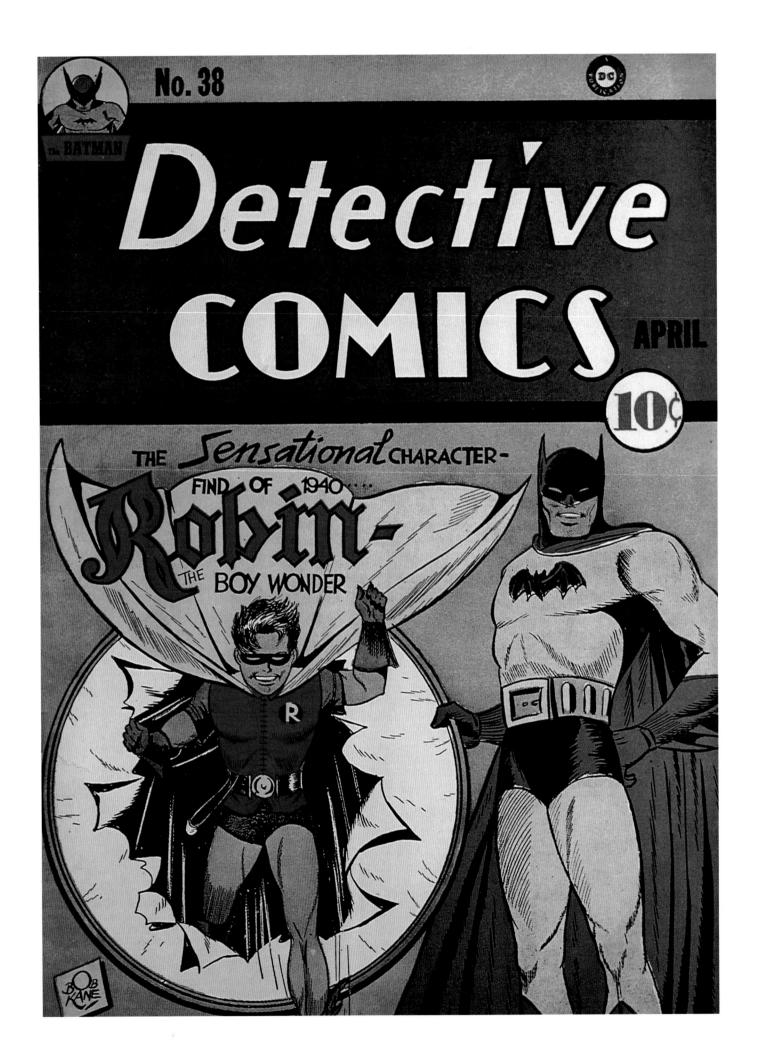

APRIL 1940; NO. 38
Cover artists: Bob Kane, Jerry Robinson

The Dynamic Duo

Batman appeared solo for almost a year before Robin was introduced, in *Detective Comics* number 38. From then on, the two crime fighters patrolled the streets of Gotham City as a team.

Lightweight yet strong-as-steel Batropes became a standard mode of transit, allowing Batman and Robin to move quickly and dramatically. As in the case of the capes, artistic license often dictated some unusual setups. Our heroes zoomed in at impossible angles from Batropes seemingly anchored to clouds (cover 81), ceilings (covers 141, 183, 191), or unseen adjacent buildings (covers 53, 125).

Whether saving upstanding citizens from lurking threats (cover 183) or rescuing each other from impending danger (cover 125), they fought ceaselessly and relentlessly to keep Gotham City from the clutches of imminent evil.

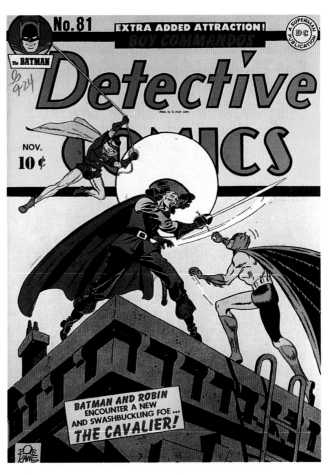

JULY 1944; NO. 89
Cover artist: Dick Sprang

NOVEMBER 1943; NO. 81
Cover artists: Bob Kane, Jerry Robinson,
George Roussos

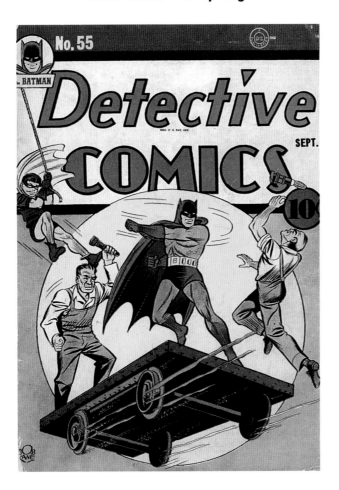

SEPTEMBER 1941; NO. 55
Cover artists: Bob Kane, Jerry Robinson

APRIL 1948; NO. 134
Cover artist: Jim Mooney

APRIL 1941; NO. 50
Cover artists: Bob Kane, Jerry Robinson

OCTOBER 1945; NO. 104
Cover artist: Dick Sprang

OCTOBER 1954; NO. 212
Cover artist: Win Mortimer

MAY 1952; NO. 183
Cover artist: Win Mortimer

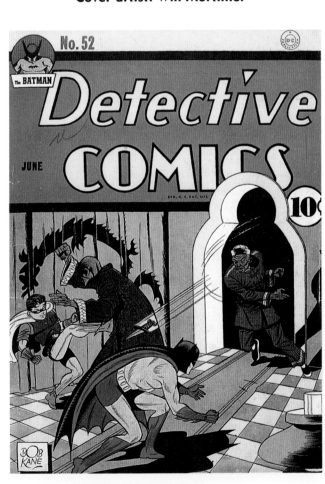

JUNE 1941; NO. 52
Cover artists: Bob Kane, Jerry Robinson

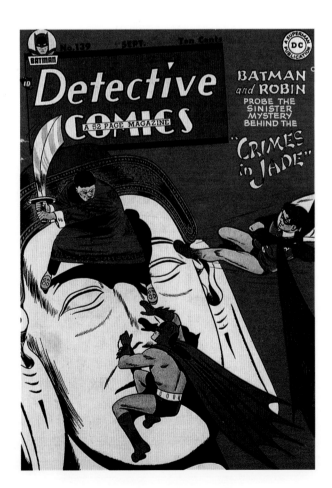

SEPTEMBER 1948; NO. 139
Cover artist: Win Mortimer

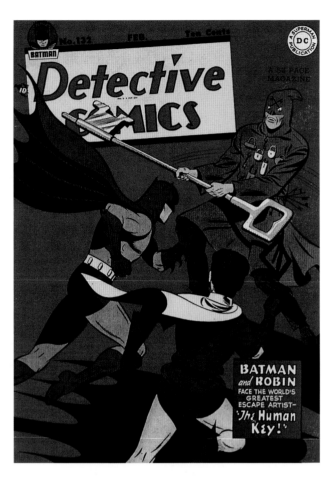

MARCH 1952; NO. 181
Cover artist: Win Mortimer

FEBRUARY 1948; NO. 132
Cover artists: Jim Mooney, Charles Paris

NOVEMBER 1953; NO. 201
Cover artist: Win Mortimer

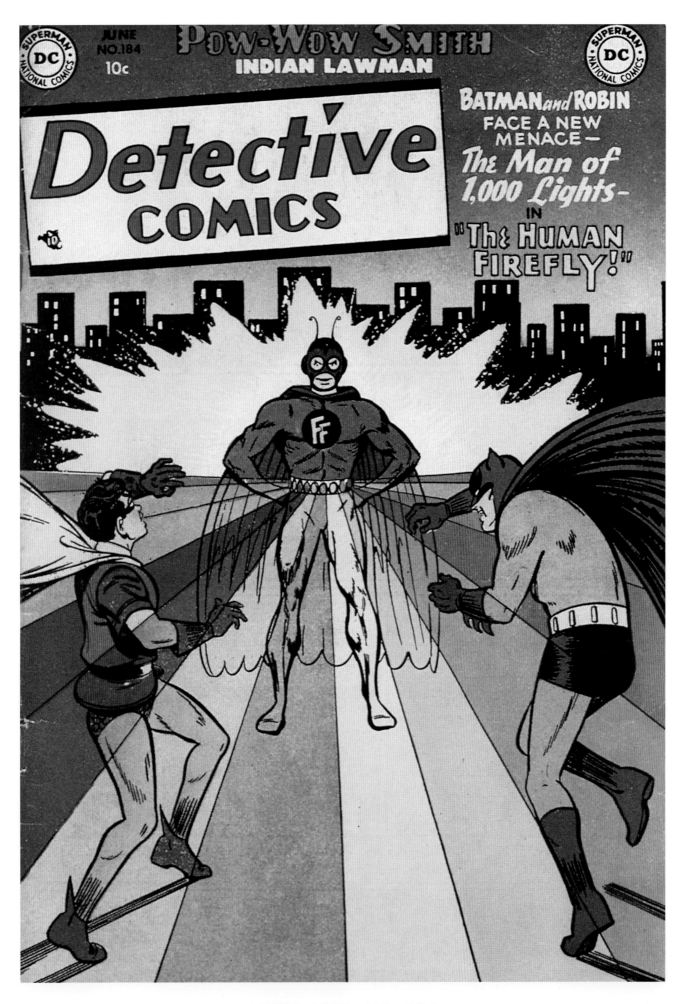

JUNE 1952; NO. 184
Cover artist: Win Mortimer

SEPTEMBER 1946; NO. 115
Cover artist: Win Mortimer

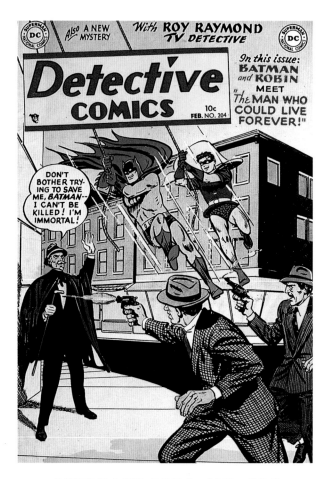

FEBRUARY 1954; NO. 204
Cover artist: Win Mortimer

38

SEPTEMBER 1949; NO. 151
Cover artists: Jim Mooney, Ray Burnley

JULY 1950; NO. 161
Cover artist: Win Mortimer

JANUARY 1953; NO. 191
Cover artist: Win Mortimer

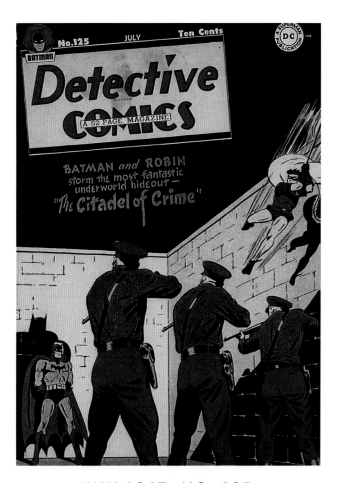

JULY 1947; NO. 125
Cover artists: Jack Burnley, Charles Paris

JUNE 1946; NO. 112
Cover artist: Win Mortimer

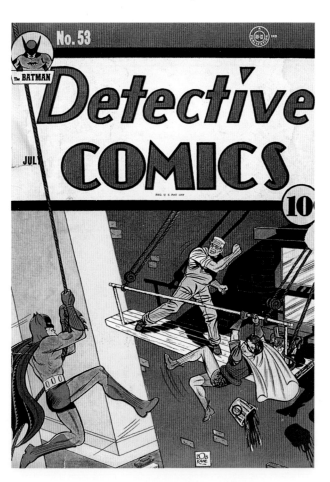

JULY 1941; NO. 53
Cover artists: Bob Kane, Jerry Robinson

JULY 1952; NO. 185
Cover artist: Win Mortimer

NOVEMBER 1948; NO. 141
Cover artists: Lew Sayre Schwartz,
Charles Paris

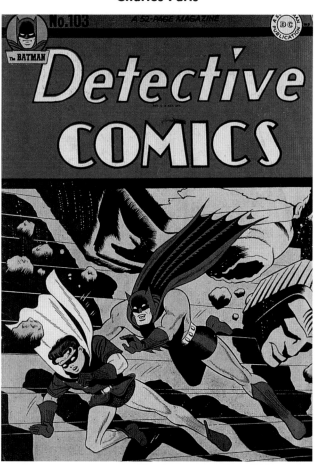

MARCH 1950; NO. 157
Cover artist: Win Mortimer

SEPTEMBER 1945; NO. 103
Cover artist: Dick Sprang

APRIL 1949; NO. 146
Cover artist: Dick Sprang

JANUARY 1947; NO. 119
Cover artist: Win Mortimer

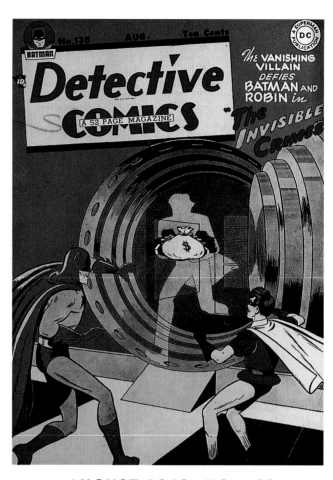

AUGUST 1948; NO. 138
Cover artist: Win Mortimer

DECEMBER 1950; NO. 166
Cover artist: Win Mortimer

APRIL 1954; NO. 206
Cover artist: Win Mortimer

JULY 1942; NO. 65
Cover artists: Jack Kirby, Joe Simon,
Jerry Robinson

JULY 1951; NO. 173
Cover artist: Win Mortimer

Dynamic Duplicates

If one Batman makes a good cover, do two make it even better? So it would seem from the covers presented in this chapter. Whether simple stand-ins (covers 84, 165) or potentially treacherous twins, multiple Batmen were not always the best thing to happen in Gotham (covers 222, 224). A replicate Robin might surface occasionally, but it was Batman who was deemed the most desirable to duplicate.

Not all impostors had evil intentions. Circus acrobat Hugo Marmon once claimed to be the original Batman (cover 195) since he had performed under the name Bat Man and used a similar costume well before Bruce Wayne ever dreamed of fighting crime. A problematic city statute was discovered prohibiting anyone but the "original Batman of Gotham City" from wearing the famous costume, but this was resolved when it was determined that our hero was indeed the first man to wear his costume within the city limits.

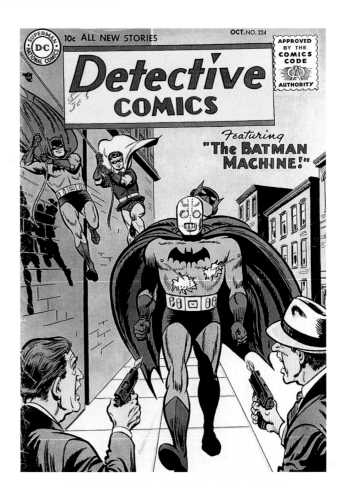

JUNE 1955; NO. 220
Cover artist: Win Mortimer

OCTOBER 1955; NO. 224
Cover artist: Win Mortimer

FEBRUARY 1944; NO. 84
Cover artist: Dick Sprang

NOVEMBER 1950; NO. 165
Cover artist: Win Mortimer

AUGUST 1955; NO. 222
Cover artist: Win Mortimer

MAY 1953; NO. 195
Cover artist: Win Mortimer

NOVEMBER 1944; NO. 93
Cover artist: Dick Sprang

All Tied Up

Of the two crime fighters, Robin was more likely to be captured and trussed up by crooks in hopes of luring Batman, since the Gotham Guardian was the one the bad guys really wanted anyway. Occasionally the Boy Wonder came to his mentor's rescue (cover 117).

The idea of being overcome by forces of evil and then forced into a seemingly inescapable doom trap (covers 93, 189, 221) became part of the Batman mythos. The origins of the doom-trap device are rooted in other elements of popular culture, particularly movie-serial cliffhangers and pulp magazines. As a staple in Batman storytelling, they showcased the Batman version of superpowers: deductive skills, heightened senses, an ability to think fast, and a properly stocked utility belt. This concept reached a parodied peak in the 1966–68 "Batman" TV series, when apparently inescapable machinations continuously dropped the Doomed Duo at death's door and served as convenient bridges between two-part episodes.

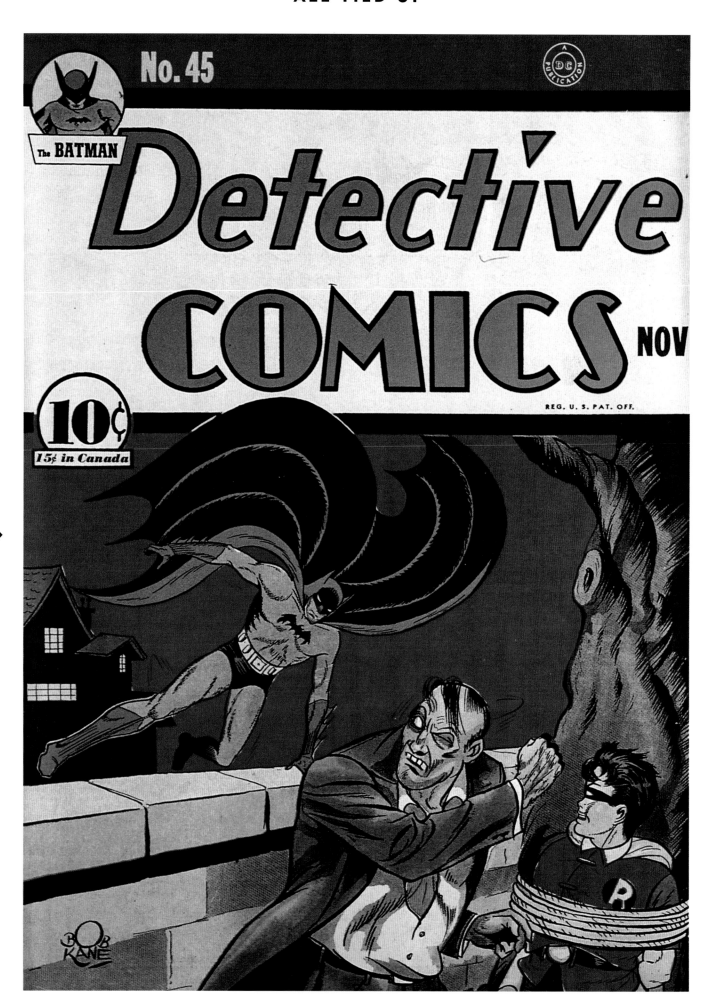

NOVEMBER 1940; NO. 45
Cover artists: Bob Kane, Jerry Robinson,
George Roussos

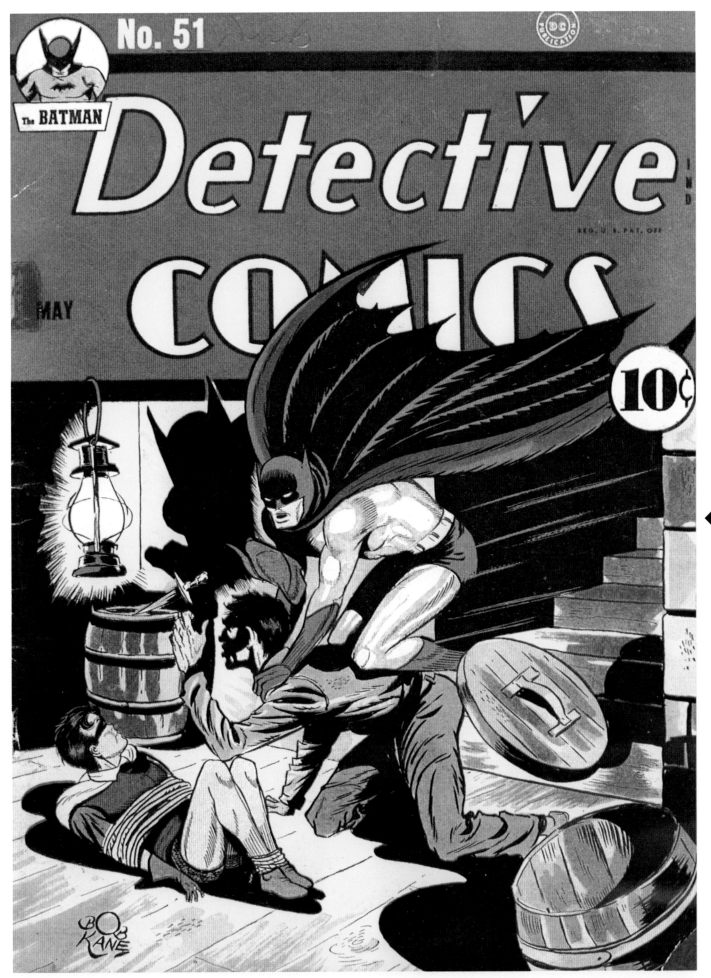

MAY 1941; NO. 51
Cover artists: Bob Kane, Jerry Robinson

MARCH 1941; NO. 49
Cover artists: Bob Kane, Jerry Robinson

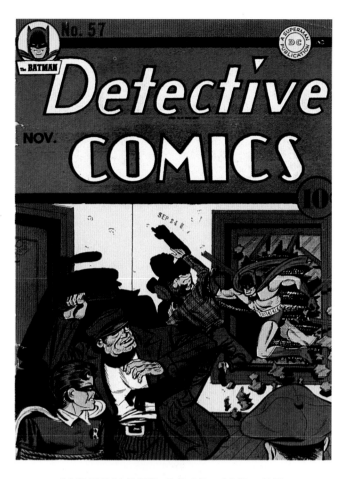

NOVEMBER 1941; NO. 57
Cover artists: Bob Kane, Jerry Robinson,
George Roussos

NOVEMBER 1952; NO. 189
Cover artist: Win Mortimer

JULY 1955; NO. 221
Cover artist: Win Mortimer

NOVEMBER 1946; NO. 117
Cover artist: Ray Burnley

JANUARY 1946; NO. 107
Cover artist: Dick Sprang

Take That!

Though Batman's utility belt contained many unique anti-crime devices, the Gotham Guardian did not use a gun (except for some rare early instances). Capturing heavily armed criminals meant quickly subduing them by administering a stiff sock in the jaw or a punch in the nose before tying them up. Every crook surely regretted seeing Batman's powerful fist at such close range, and even Batman himself must have suffered some sore knuckles. Perhaps that's why the Dynamic Duo occasionally chose to spare their hands, utilizing instead a swift kick (covers 36, 47), a headlock (cover 63), a water hose (cover 97), or even a football (cover 82).

FEBRUARY 1940; NO. 36
Cover artist: Bob Kane

MAY 1940; NO. 39
Cover artists: Bob Kane, Jerry Robinson

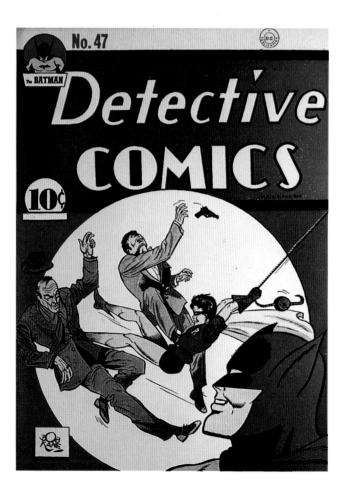

JANUARY 1941; NO. 47
Cover artists: Bob Kane, Jerry Robinson,
George Roussos

APRIL 1944; NO. 86
Cover artist: Dick Sprang

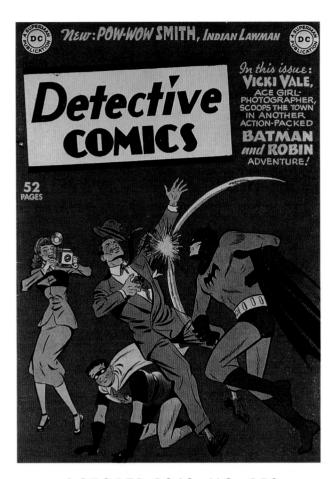

OCTOBER 1949; NO. 152
Cover artist: Win Mortimer

JUNE 1948; NO. 136
Cover artist: Dick Sprang

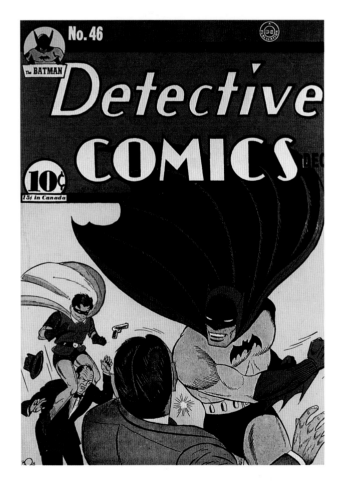

DECEMBER 1940; NO. 46
Cover artists: Bob Kane, Jerry Robinson,
George Roussos

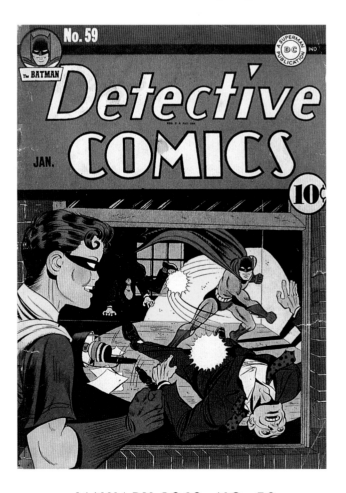

JANUARY 1942; NO. 59
Cover artists: Bob Kane, Jerry Robinson,
George Roussos

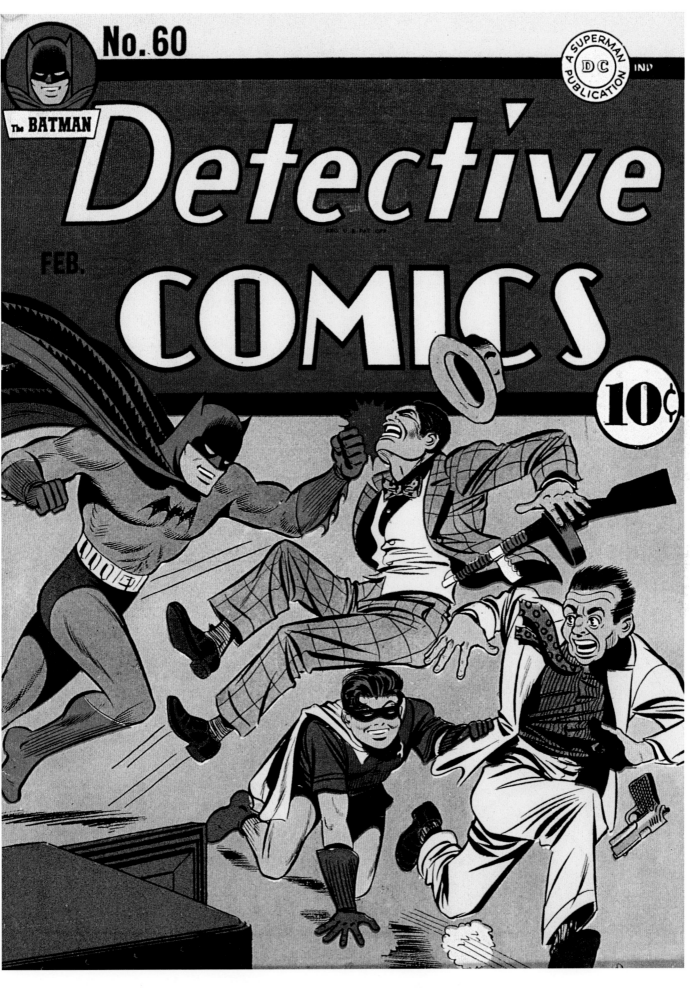

FEBRUARY 1942; NO. 60
Cover artists: Fred Ray, Jerry Robinson

MARCH 1945; NO. 97
Cover artist: Dick Sprang

DECEMBER 1943; NO. 82
Cover artists: Bob Kane, Jerry Robinson

JUNE 1944; NO. 88
Cover artist: Dick Sprang

61

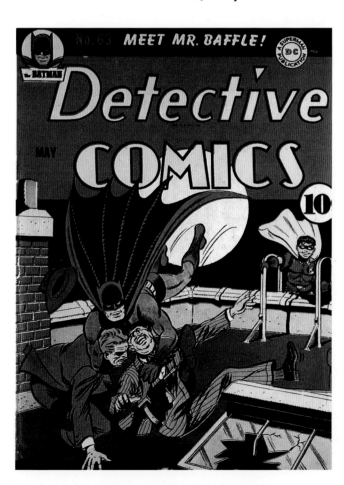

MAY 1942; NO. 63
Cover artists: Fred Ray, Jerry Robinson

APRIL 1945; NO. 98
Cover artist: Dick Sprang

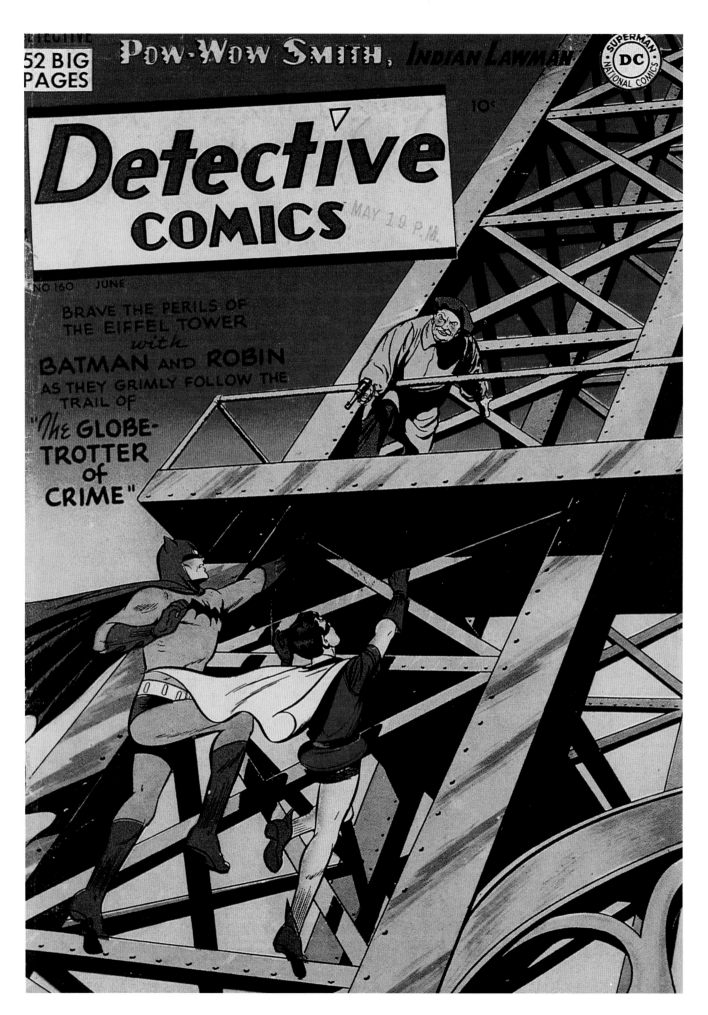

JUNE 1950; NO. 160
Cover artist: Win Mortimer

Aimless Villains

Criminals in comics have traditionally had astonishingly poor aim with firearms, often missing their targets at point-blank range. One wonders if they had ever used a gun before. Or were they shooting blanks? Batman and Robin could have been shot and killed many times, but fortunately for our heroes, their opposition couldn't hit a barn with a howitzer at twenty paces, thereby ensuring many more adventures, with some close calls thrown in to keep things interesting.

In the 1989 feature film *Batman*, the Gotham Guardian wore a heavy, essentially bullet-proof costume. But in the comics, Batman was never completely bullet-proof, and indeed was close to death from gunshot wounds in several stories.

MAY 1949; NO. 147
Cover artist: Dick Sprang

FEBRUARY 1949; NO. 144
Cover artist: Dick Sprang

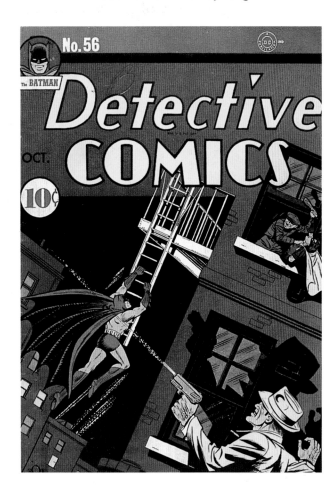

OCTOBER 1941; NO. 56
Cover artists: Bob Kane, Jerry Robinson

MARCH 1947; NO. 121
Cover artists: Jack Burnley, Charles Paris

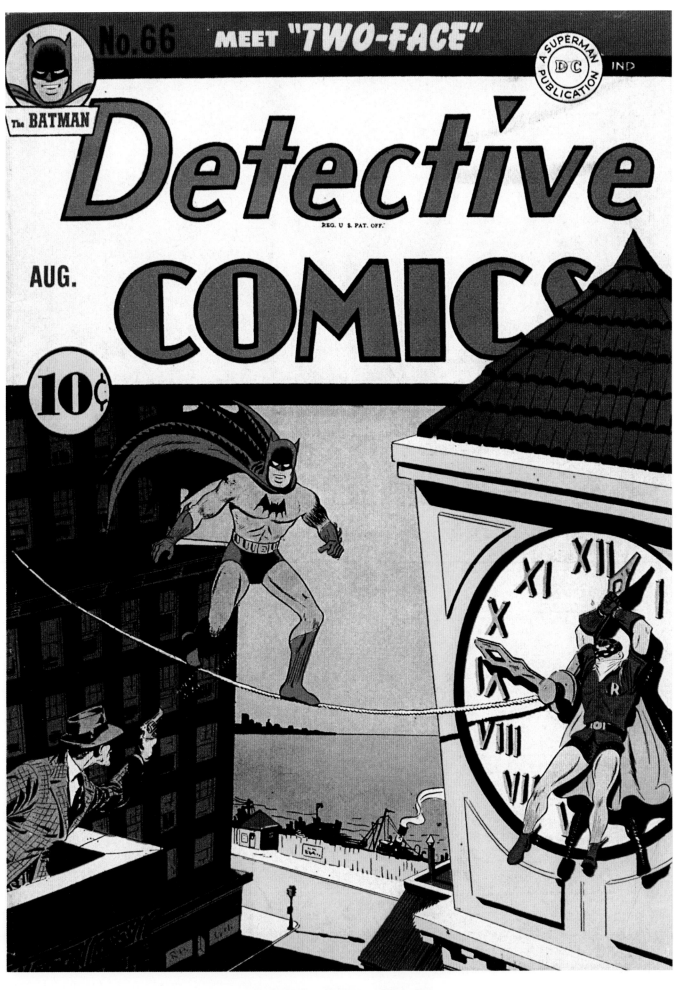

AUGUST 1942; NO. 66
Cover artists: Jerry Robinson, George Roussos

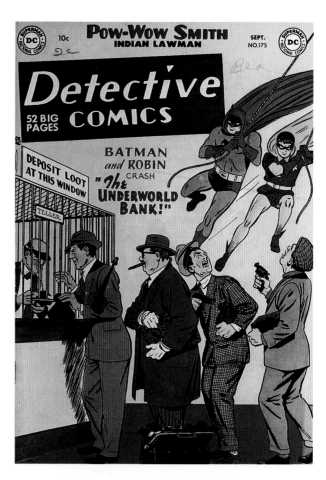

JANUARY 1944; NO. 83
Cover artist: Jack Burnley

SEPTEMBER 1951; NO. 175
Cover artist: Win Mortimer

JANUARY 1945; NO. 95
Cover artists: Bob Kane, George Roussos

MAY 1947; NO. 123
Cover artists: Jack Burnley, Charles Paris

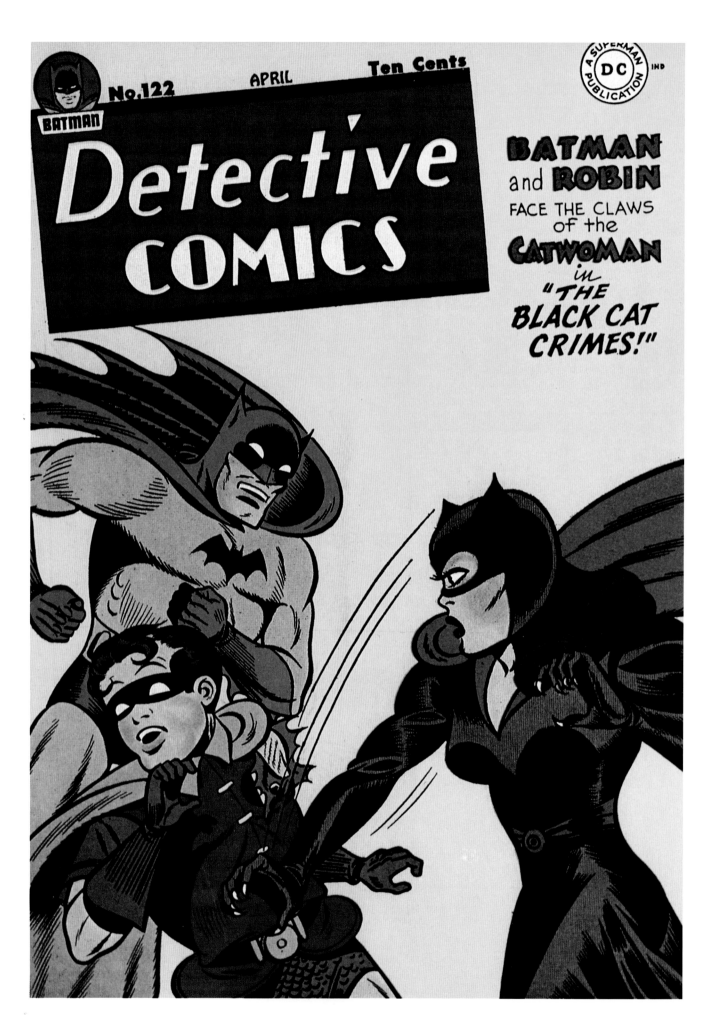

APRIL 1947; NO. 122
Cover artists: Bob Kane, Ray Burnley

Archenemies

Along with the Joker, the classic criminals seen here comprise the five most familiar Batman villains. With the exception of Two-Face, these archenemies were also popularized by the 1960s "Batman" TV program. This is especially true of the Riddler, since only two of his adventures were published during the 1940s.

Starting out as a jewel thief, Catwoman soon became a love interest for Batman. Feline imagery dominated her behavior—she drove a kitty car, brandished a cat-o'-nine-tails, and, in her alter ego of Selina Kyle, owned a pet shop.

The Penguin was another early development, first appearing in *Detective Comics* issue 58. Although the Penguin's crimes have involved birds, he is best known for his diabolically inventive umbrellas.

First appearing in *Detective Comics* issue 66, Two-Face surfaced occasionally during the Golden Age. His duality extended beyond his face and clothes to include the use of twos in his crimes (such as striking at two o'clock on cover 187) and in his hideout, which had two of everything.

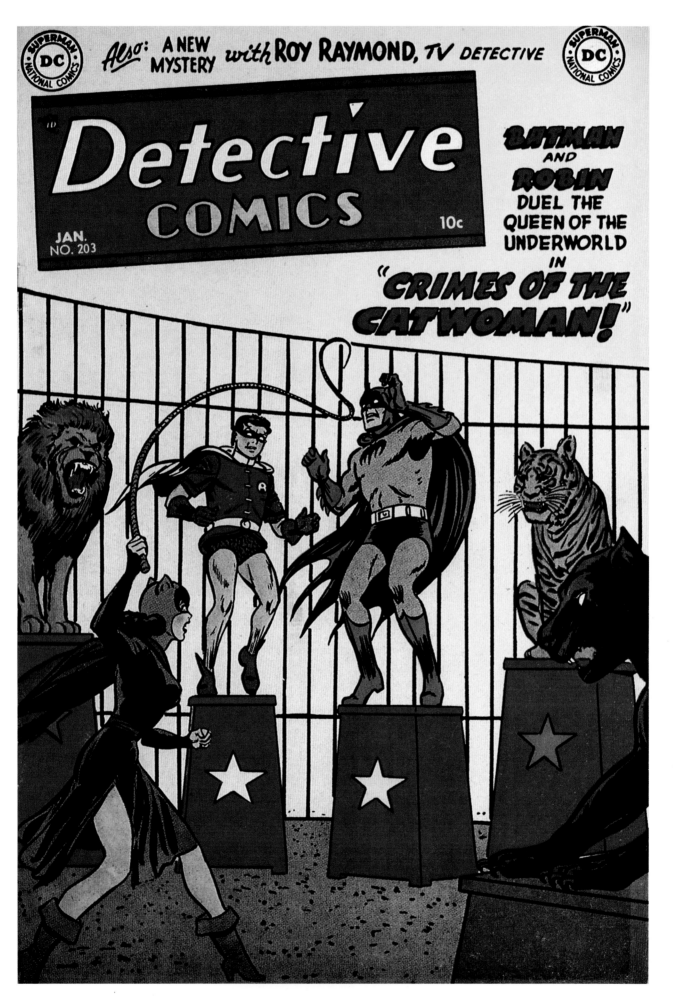

JANUARY 1954; NO. 203
Cover artist: Win Mortimer

SEPTEMBER 1954; NO. 211
Cover artist: Win Mortimer

MAY 1951; NO. 171
Cover artist: Win Mortimer

AUGUST 1947; NO. 126
Cover artists: Jack Burnley, Win Mortimer

SEPTEMBER 1942; NO. 67
Cover artist: Jerry Robinson

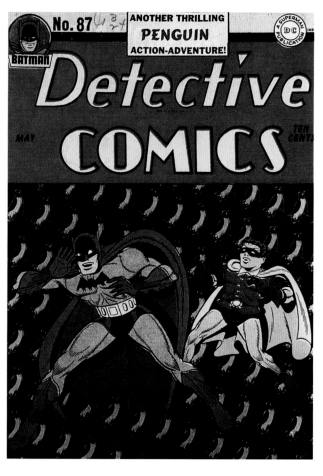

MAY 1944; NO. 87
Cover artist: Dick Sprang

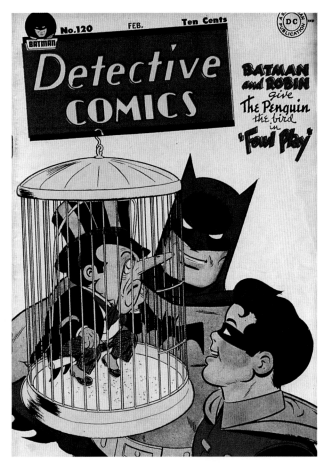

FEBRUARY 1947; NO. 120
Cover artist: Win Mortimer

MAY 1945; NO. 99
Cover artist: Dick Sprang

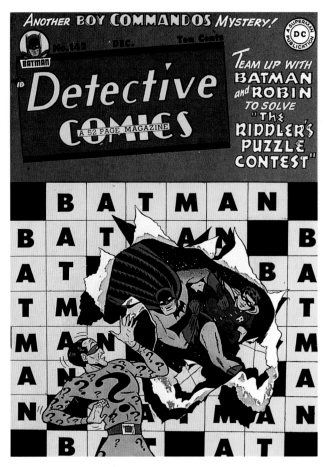

DECEMBER 1948; NO. 142
Cover artists: Dick Sprang, Charles Paris

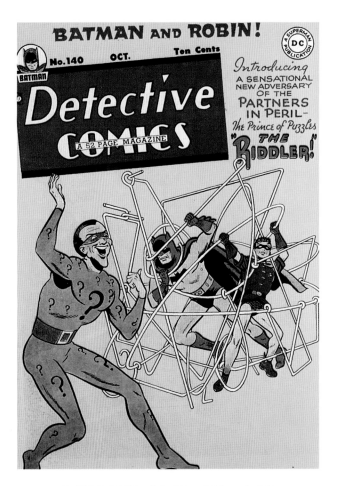

OCTOBER 1948; NO. 140
Cover artist: Win Mortimer

OCTOBER 1943; NO. 80
Cover artists: Bob Kane, Jerry Robinson,
George Roussos

SEPTEMBER 1952; NO. 187
Cover artist: Win Mortimer

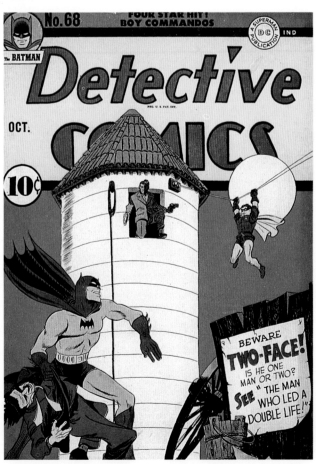

OCTOBER 1942; NO. 68
Cover artist: Jerry Robinson

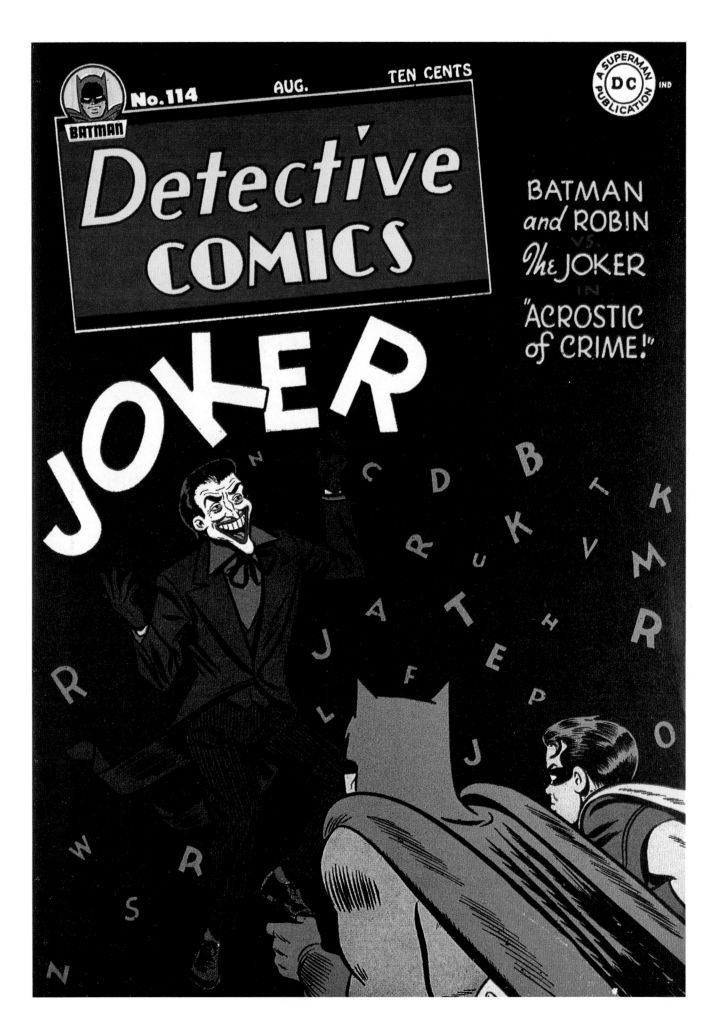

AUGUST 1946; NO. 114
Cover artist: Win Mortimer

The Joker's on YOU

Described in *Batman* number 4 as the "cleverest and the most dangerous criminal in the annals of crime," the Joker's spine-chilling laughter, chalk-white skin, green hair, and evil grin make him one of the most memorable villains in Batman's Rogues Gallery. The cunning Clown Prince of Crime is one of the Caped Crusader's most persistent archenemies, having first appeared in *Batman* number 1 (Spring 1940). The Grim Jester's *Detective Comics* cover debut was issue 40; the more enduring visualization of the Joker first appeared on cover 62.

Batman's most famous nemesis wins as most frequent cover culprit, his ghastly grin gracing more covers in this volume than any other villain. Even the nefarious Penguin is a distant second, with only six cover appearances to the Joker's formidable eighteen.

AUGUST 1945; NO. 102
Cover artist: Dick Sprang

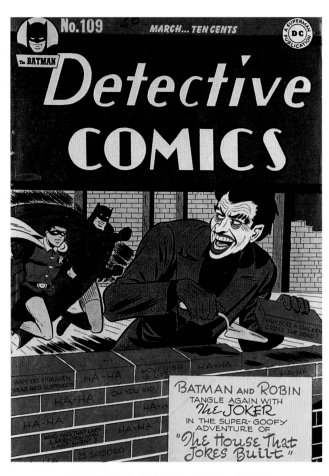

MARCH 1946; NO. 109
Cover artist: Jack Burnley, Ray Burnley

SEPTEMBER 1944; NO. 91
Cover artist: Dick Sprang

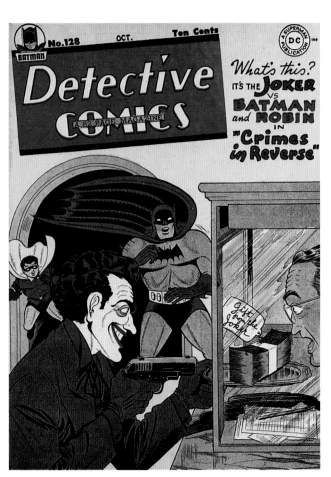

OCTOBER 1947; NO. 128
Cover artist: Dick Sprang

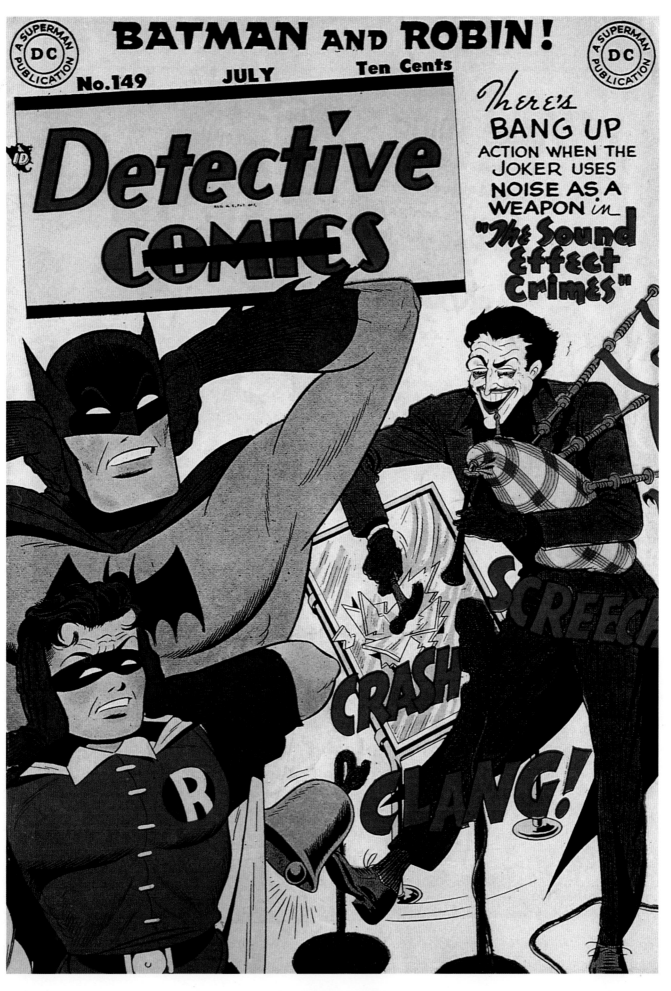

JULY 1949; NO. 149
Cover artist: Dick Sprang

JULY 1948; NO. 137
Cover artists: Bob Kane, Charles Paris

JUNE 1947; NO. 124
Cover artists: Bob Kane, Charles Paris

DECEMBER 1946; NO. 118
Cover artist: Dick Sprang

FEBRUARY 1952; NO. 180
Cover artist: Win Mortimer

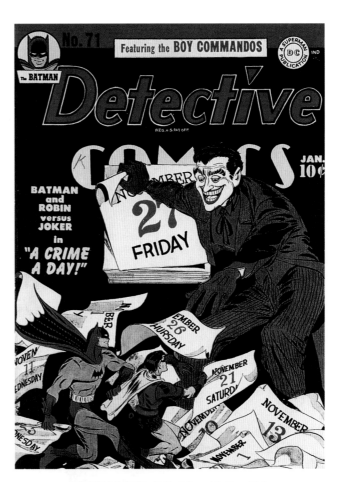

JANUARY 1943; NO. 71
Cover artist: Jerry Robinson

MARCH 1953; NO. 193
Cover artist: Win Mortimer

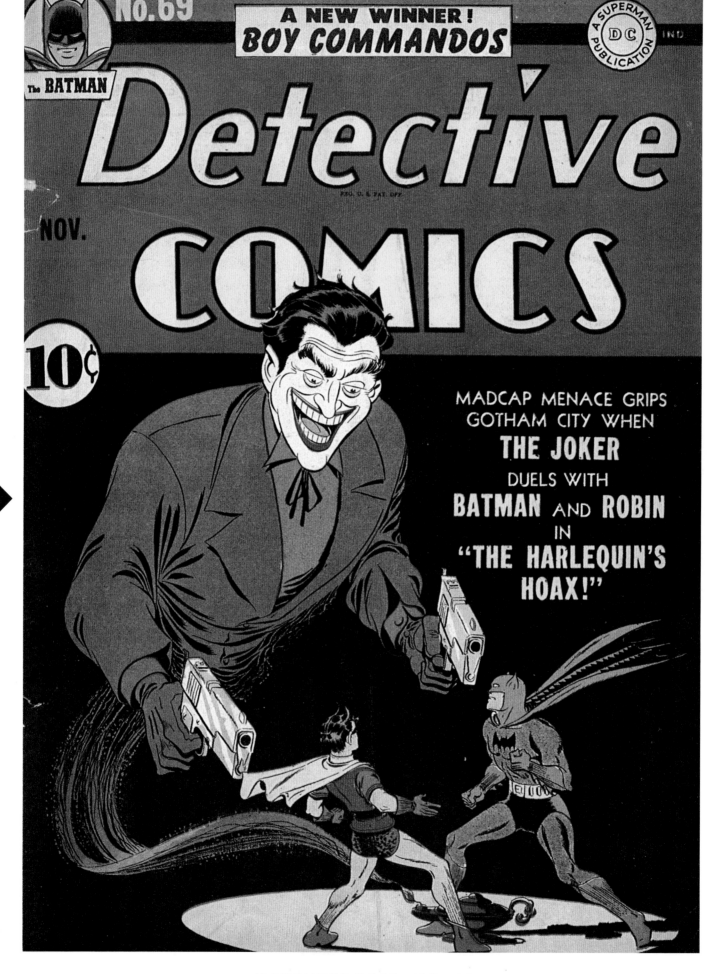

NOVEMBER 1942; NO. 69
Cover artist: Jerry Robinson

JUNE 1940; NO. 40
Cover artists: Bob Kane, Jerry Robinson

APRIL 1942; NO. 62
Cover artist: Jerry Robinson

JUNE 1943; NO. 76
Cover artist: Jerry Robinson

MARCH 1944; NO. 85
Cover artist: Dick Sprang

83

MARCH 1942; NO. 61
Cover artists: Bob Kane, Jerry Robinson,
George Roussos

Gotham Guardian

The image of a huge, omniscient Batman watching over Gotham City is a classic take on the character. Unlike Superman and other strange visitors from other planets, the Gotham Guardian was just a regular guy. He could not fly, was not invulnerable, and did not have X-ray vision or superhuman strength. Yet Batman had his own versions of such powers. His amazing deductive abilities allowed him to puzzle out the most complex riddles and clues dropped by villains. His technical expertise—in apparently everything—enabled him to construct extraordinary vehicles, computers, and other crime-fighting devices. Laboratory know-how kept his utility belt well supplied, and his daily workout in the gym kept his athletic prowess in peak form. Plus he had that uncanny knack for being in the right place at exactly the right time, ready to battle evildoers wherever they might strike next.

SEPTEMBER 1939; NO. 31
Cover artist: Bob Kane

JANUARY 1955; NO. 215
Cover artists: Sheldon Moldoff, Charles Paris

AUGUST 1940; NO. 42
Cover artists: Bob Kane, Jerry Robinson

87

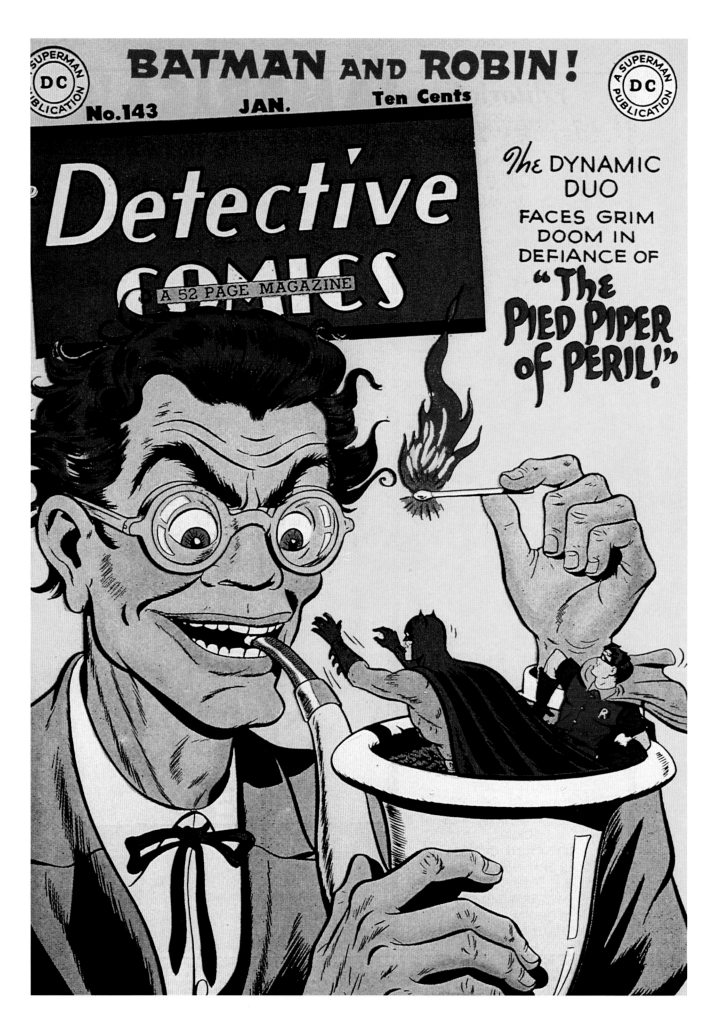

JANUARY 1949; NO. 143
Cover artist: Jim Mooney

Larger Than Life

Just as a movie poster might exaggerate elements of a story or highlight an action-packed sequence to entice viewers, comic-book covers have always been designed for visual impact. Graphically distorted and stylized villains lent a heightened aura of menace. The symbolism and expressionism of these covers served as a lure to the exciting stories inside, even if the exact scenes were often not to be found in the story itself. Oversized props also became integral to many stories, thanks to writer Bill Finger. His concept of giant devices was subsequently adopted by other Batman writers, becoming crucial to Batman storytelling.

MARCH 1943; NO. 73
Cover artists: Bob Kane, Jerry Robinson

SEPTEMBER 1947; NO. 127
Cover artist: Charles Paris

FEBRUARY 1951; NO. 168
Cover artists: Lew Sayre Schwartz,
Charles Paris

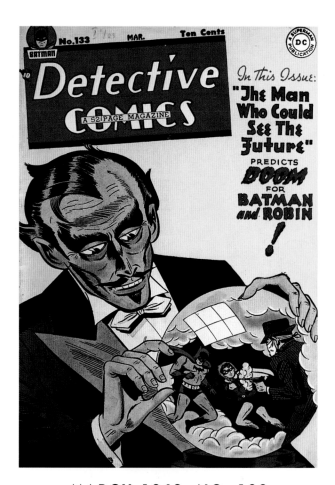

MARCH 1948; NO. 133
Cover artists: Lew Sayre Schwartz, Bob Kane,
Charles Paris

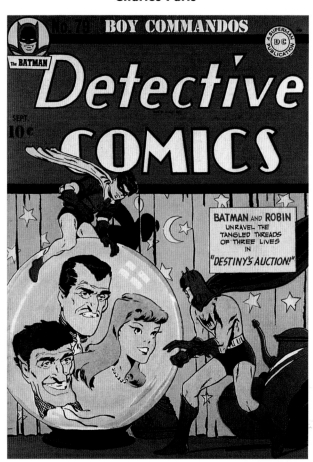

SEPTEMBER 1943; NO. 79
Cover artist: Jerry Robinson

FEBRUARY 1943; NO. 72
Cover artist: Jerry Robinson

JANUARY 1948; NO. 131
Cover artists: Lew Sayre Schwartz, Bob Kane,
Charles Paris

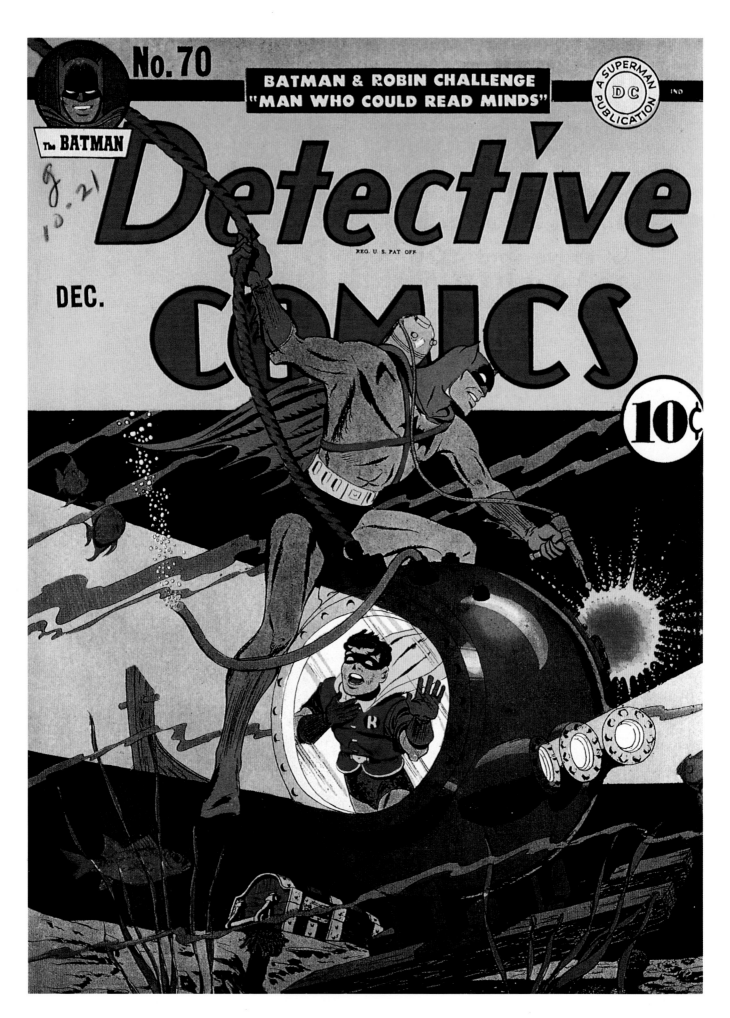

DECEMBER 1942; NO. 70
Cover artist: Jerry Robinson

Doom in the Depths

Batman and Robin never needed to venture far to find danger—plenty of it was always to be found on dry land in Gotham City. But sometimes our heroes encountered peril of the watery kind. Whether tracking a criminal through the city sewers (covers 94, 145), combatting crooks aboard a vessel on the high seas (covers 58, 90, 133), or fighting for their lives in the ocean depths (cover 70), the Caped Crusaders managed to pursue criminals whenever and wherever they attempted to escape.

The Dynamic Duo might seem to have the upper hand in most situations, but they have also found themselves in some deadly traps, seemingly headed for a watery grave (covers 100, 189). Other adventures (covers 202, 221) have seen them shoved into the water with their hands tied but, naturally, utility belts still intact.

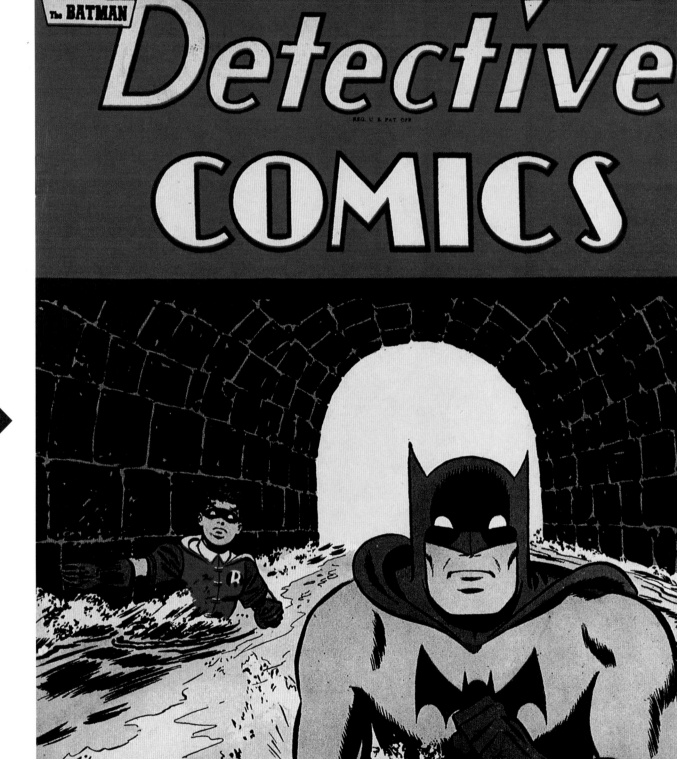

DECEMBER 1944; NO. 94
Cover artist: Jerry Robinson

JUNE 1945; NO. 100
Cover artist: Dick Sprang

DECEMBER 1949; NO. 154
Cover artists: Jim Mooney, Charles Paris

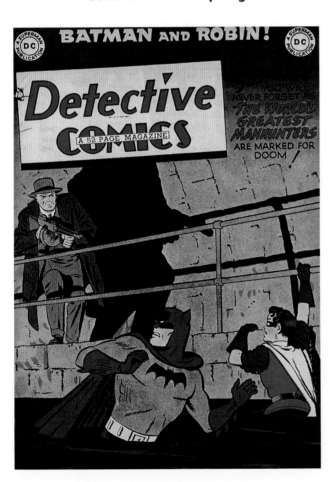

MARCH 1949; NO. 145
Cover artist: Win Mortimer

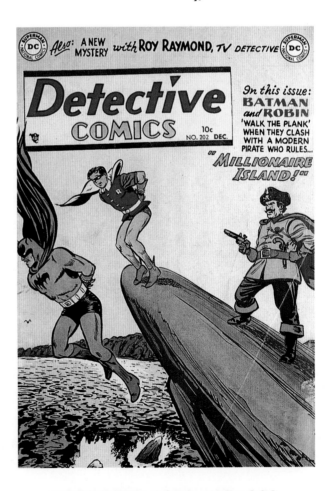

DECEMBER 1953; NO. 202
Cover artist: Win Mortimer

JULY 1955; NO. 221
Cover artist: Win Mortimer

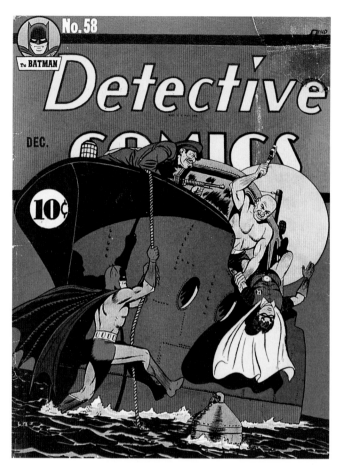

DECEMBER 1941; NO. 58
Cover artists: Fred Ray, Jerry Robinson

AUGUST 1944; NO. 90
Cover artist: Dick Sprang

NOVEMBER 1952; NO. 189
Cover artist: Win Mortimer

JULY 1946; NO. 113
Cover artist: Dick Sprang

SEPTEMBER 1939; NO. 31
Cover artist: Bob Kane

Bat Moon Rising

Moons can be found on a number of Batman covers, but monstrously large lunar orbs are unique to Batman's earliest adventures. For several years both covers and stories depicted his nocturnal hunts for the criminal denizens of Gotham City's alleys and shadowy underworld. This Batman was by necessity a night fighter, a creature of the night, the Dark Knight. An oversized full moon quickly and effectively helped define the mood and provided a striking graphic device against which to silhouette figures.

Eventually Batman was depicted more frequently in daylight or in interior setups, so the moons waned. The introduction of the Bat-Signal may have contributed as well, since it looked most effective on cloudy skies.

OCTOBER 1944; NO. 92
Cover artist: Dick Sprang

JULY 1940; NO. 41
Cover artists: Bob Kane, Jerry Robinson

MAY 1942; NO. 63
Cover artists: Fred Ray, Jerry Robinson

SEPTEMBER 1940; NO. 43
Cover artists: Bob Kane, Jerry Robinson

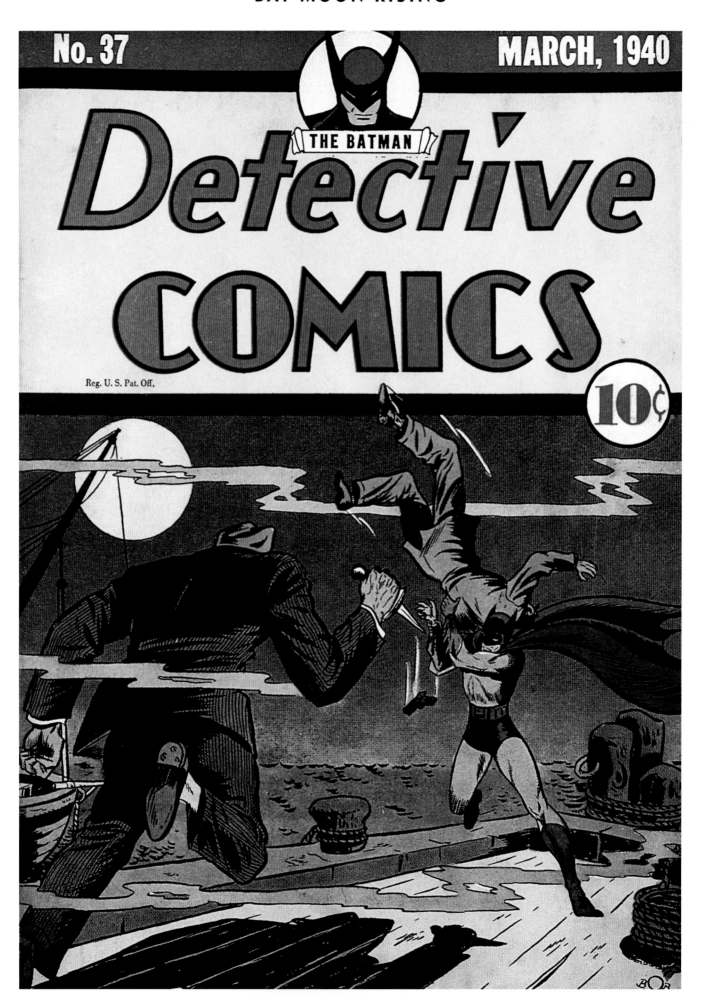

MARCH 1940; NO. 37
Cover artist: Bob Kane

MAY 1943; NO. 75
Cover artists: Bob Kane, George Roussos

MARCH 1941; NO. 49
Cover artists: Bob Kane, Jerry Robinson

OCTOBER 1940; NO. 44
Cover artists: Bob Kane, Jerry Robinson,
George Roussos

FEBRUARY 1946; NO. 108
Cover artist: George Roussos

AUGUST 1949; NO. 150
Cover artist: Win Mortimer

The Bat-Signal

Described in issue 164 as an "eerie finger of brilliant light, which regularly chills the underworld as it sets in motion the Dynamic Duo," the Bat-Signal was first employed in *Detective Comics* number 60, although it didn't make the cover until issue 150. Essentially a large searchlight located on the roof of police headquarters, the device can penetrate fog and smoke, has a bullet-proof glass lens, and uses super-carbon arc filaments. When it projects its silhouette of a giant bat on a cloudy night sky, Batman and Robin may respond in a variety of ways. They may report directly to Commissioner Gordon for instructions (cover 150), follow the direction of the signal (cover 186), or contact police headquarters by two-way radio. Batman's fame is worldwide—the Bat-Signal can even be found in England (cover 196).

MAY 1951; NO. 171
Cover artist: Win Mortimer

OCTOBER 1950; NO. 164
Cover artist: Win Mortimer

JUNE 1953; NO. 196
Cover artist: Win Mortimer

AUGUST 1952; NO. 186
Cover artist: Win Mortimer

JULY 1953; NO. 197
Cover artist: Win Mortimer

Planes, Trains, and Batmobiles

The Dynamic Duo's exploits have occurred in a variety of locations, and the two have generally relied on their own means of transportation so they could avail themselves of hidden crime-fighting devices, as detailed in the Batmobile plans on cover 156. The Batmobile is undoubtedly the most famous of their vehicles, although Batman had no such vehicle in his earliest adventures. The Batplane, introduced in *Detective Comics* number 31 as a Batgyro, evolved into an actual plane, and after undergoing numerous technological changes became a jet.

When the treasurer of the Wayne Motor Company disappeared with millions of dollars, Bruce Wayne needed quick cash. Naturally this situation affected Batman, who was forced to sell the Batmobile (cover 105). Alfred helped out, earning $3.75 mowing lawns, and Dick Grayson pitched in with his paper-route money. Eventually the absconding treasurer was caught and financial order restored to Wayne Manor.

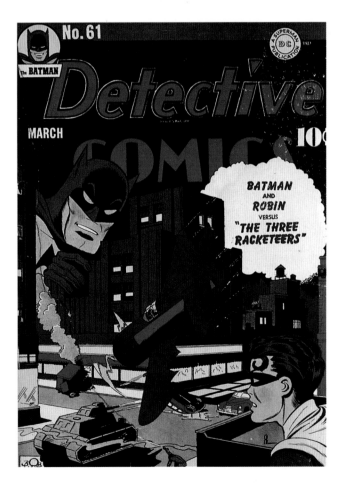

JUNE 1951; NO. 172
Cover artist: Win Mortimer

OCTOBER 1953; NO. 200
Cover artist: Win Mortimer

MARCH 1942; NO. 61
Cover artists: Bob Kane, Jerry Robinson,
George Roussos

FEBRUARY 1946; NO. 108
Cover artist: George Roussos

MAY 1949; NO. 147
Cover artist: Dick Sprang

FEBRUARY 1955; NO. 216
Cover artist: Win Mortimer

JUNE 1942; NO. 64
Cover artist: Jerry Robinson

FEBRUARY 1945; NO. 96
Cover artists: Jack Burnley, George Roussos

AUGUST 1950; NO. 162
Cover artist: Win Mortimer

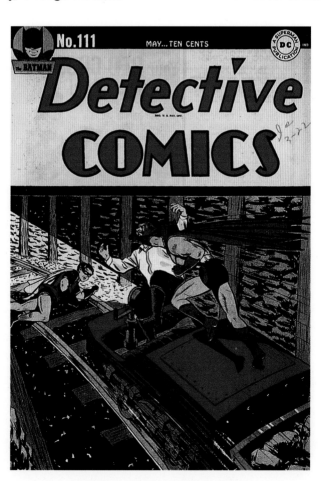

MAY 1946; NO. 111
Cover artist: Win Mortimer

NOVEMBER 1945; NO. 105
Cover artists: Jack Burnley, Charles Paris

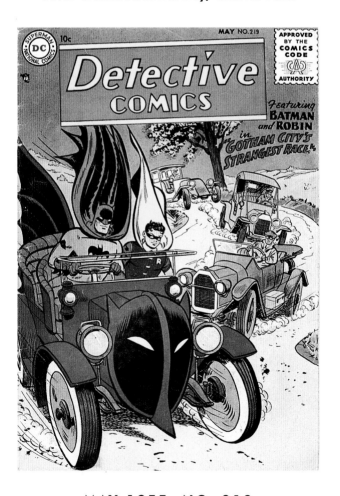

MAY 1955; NO. 219
Cover artist: Win Mortimer

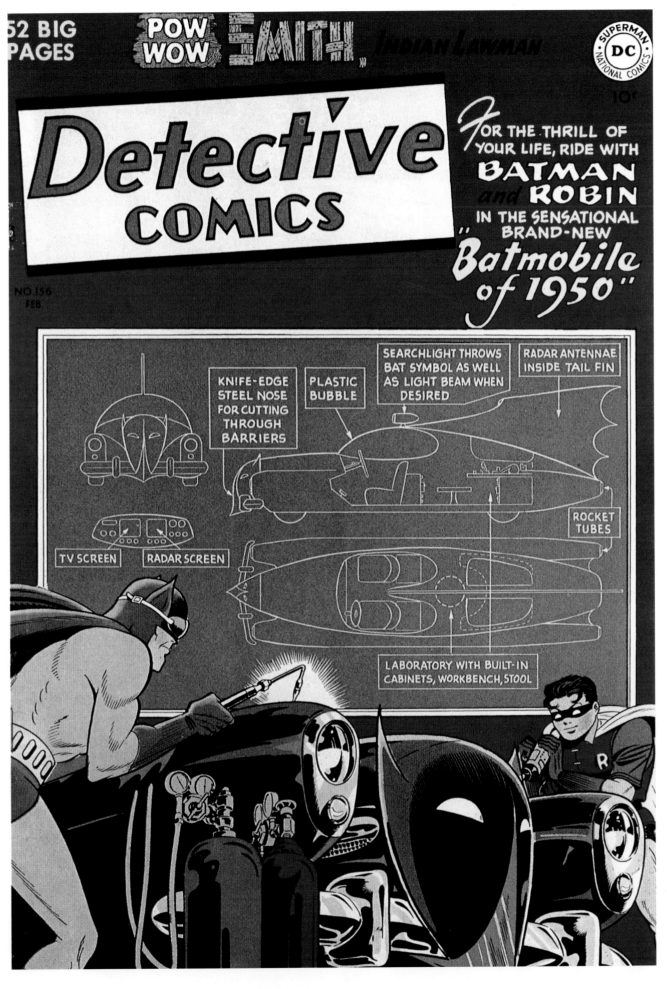

FEBRUARY 1950; NO. 156
Cover artist: Dick Sprang

MARCH 1954; NO. 205
Cover artist: Win Mortimer

The Batcave

Batman actually worked without a Batcave for a number of years. He did have a hidden hangar for the Batplane, and later a deserted barn connected to the Wayne mansion by a secret underground passageway. The modern notion of the Batcave as a natural subterranean cavern was ultimately defined in 1948.

Batcave activities often revolved around some problem or challenge for the Dynamic Duo as they utilized a vast array of sophisticated equipment (cover 192). At one point, they traveled back in time (cover 205) to discover that the cave had originally been used in the seventeenth century by a white spy masquerading as an Indian—a man of two identities, just like Batman.

In order to free Robin from criminal hands, Batman was once forced to agree not to set foot in Gotham City for one week. The intrepid crime fighter kept his word, and battled crime from a flying Batcave (cover 186), an airborne vehicle complete with TV monitors, electromagnets, and other equipment borrowed from the real Batcave.

APRIL 1950; NO. 158
Cover artist: Win Mortimer

NOVEMBER 1951; NO. 177
Cover artist: Win Mortimer

SEPTEMBER 1955; NO. 223
Cover artist: Win Mortimer

AUGUST 1952; NO. 186
Cover artist: Win Mortimer

FEBRUARY 1953; NO. 192
Cover artist: Win Mortimer

OCTOBER 1952; NO. 188
Cover artist: Win Mortimer

MARCH 1955; NO. 217
Cover artist: Win Mortimer

MAY 1950; NO. 159
Cover artist: Win Mortimer

The Man Behind the Mask

The underworld is perpetually seeking to unmask the super-heroes who threaten their livelihood, and Batman certainly had his share of enemies relentlessly bent on revealing his secret identity. It was more than idle curiosity that motivated these villains: they hoped to render the Gotham Guardian useless by threatening his friends and relatives. With his loved ones held hostage, they reasoned, Batman could be held at bay. Thus millionaire socialite Bruce Wayne and his ward, Dick Grayson, continually strove to conceal their alter egos and even conceived certain ploys to confuse the identity seekers. Bruce Wayne, for example, signs his name with his right hand, while Batman signs with his left. But however careful they were, determined criminals occasionally penetrated the mystery (covers 159, 194). Even Batman himself once forgot his own identity after being exposed to amnesia gas (see cover 190 on page 132).

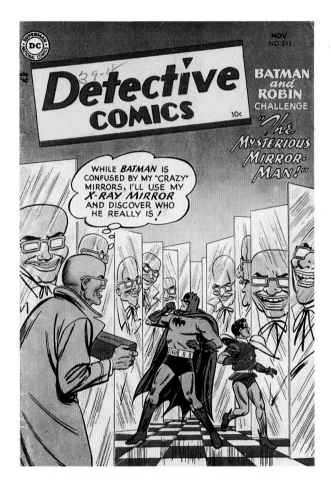

APRIL 1953; NO. 194
Cover artist: Win Mortimer

NOVEMBER 1954; NO. 213
Cover artist: Win Mortimer

124

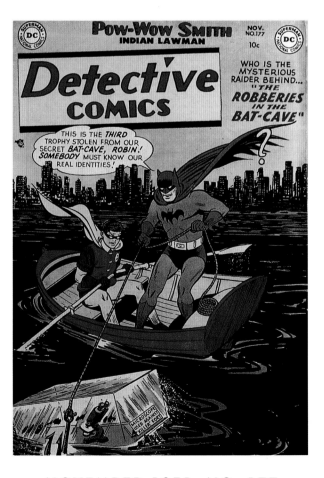

APRIL 1951; NO. 170
Cover artist: Win Mortimer

NOVEMBER 1951; NO. 177
Cover artist: Win Mortimer

JANUARY 1952; NO. 179
Cover artist: Win Mortimer

JANUARY 1950; NO. 155
Cover artist: Win Mortimer

JANUARY 1940; NO. 35
Cover artist: Bob Kane

Mad Scientists

Batman was not the only genius in Gotham with a chemistry set. Demented masterminds also required a place to hang their dangerous hats, plot their dastardly deeds, and concoct deadly new formulas. Sometimes their electronic wizardry even rivaled the Batcave's own (cover 209). A danger to society as a whole and to Batman in particular, the twisted scientist was among the most likely to figure out Batman's secret identity and the location of the Batcave, thus destroying the Caped Crusader's career plans.

Names alone often hint at their diabolical personae: Professor Hugo Strange, Professor Radium, Professor Zero, Dr. Death, Dr. Doom, Dr. No-Face, and the Inventor. Of course, none of these characters were successful in defeating Batman, but they usually proved more challenging than the average bank robber.

JULY 1954; NO. 209
Cover artist: Win Mortimer

JULY 1943; NO. 77
Cover artists: Bob Kane, George Roussos

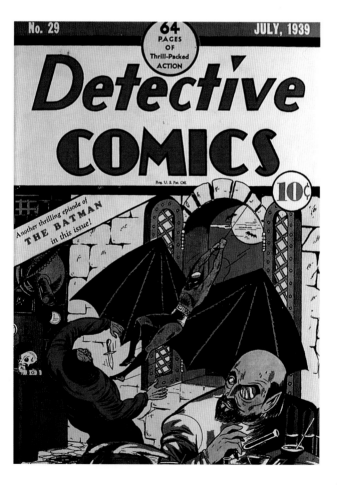

JULY 1939; NO. 29
Cover artist: Bob Kane

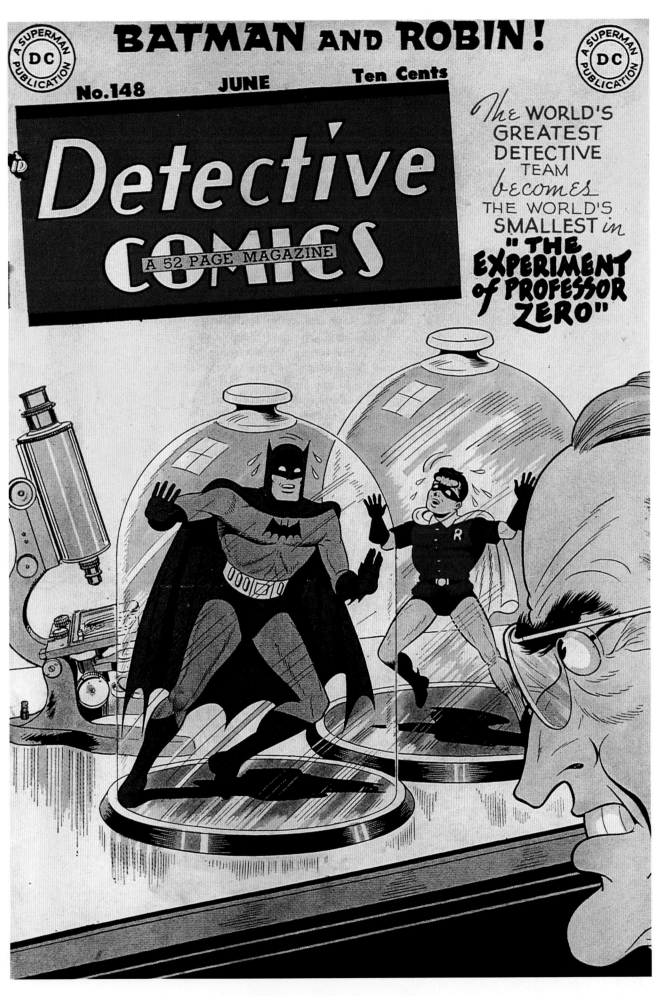

JUNE 1949; NO. 148
Cover artist: Dick Sprang

SEPTEMBER 1950; NO. 163
Cover artist: Win Mortimer

Altered Ego

Batman generally maintained a predictable but rigorous routine of detective work, research, and pursuit as he worked to capture criminals. But playing the good guy all the time could get a bit monotonous, so to keep things lively the creators turned the tables every so often. Thus Batman occasionally found himself in very unusual circumstances, facing atypical activities, or being controlled by a criminal mind. He has been overmastered by a villainous brain (cover 210), been afflicted with total amnesia (cover 190), been turned into an easily manipulated puppet (cover 182), been rendered invisible (cover 199), and done time as a human bomb (cover 163). He has even appeared to experience full-blown superpowers (cover 153) when he donned Professor Carl Wilde's mechanical Batwings and emulated a real bat. Such transformations were of course eventually overcome, and Batman always reverted to his old reliable self, ready to face another day of fighting crime.

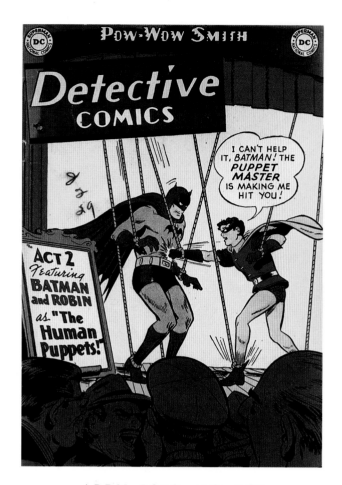

APRIL 1952; NO. 182
Cover artist: Win Mortimer

DECEMBER 1952; NO. 190
Cover artist: Win Mortimer

AUGUST 1954; NO. 210
Cover artist: Win Mortimer

NOVEMBER 1949; NO. 153
Cover artist: Dick Sprang

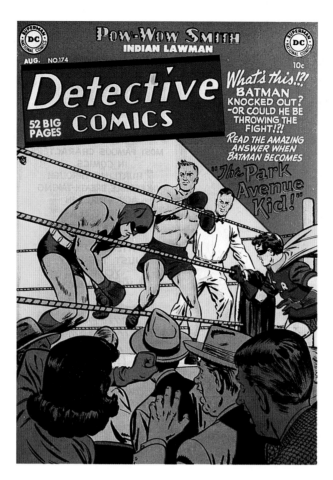

AUGUST 1951; NO. 174
Cover artist: Win Mortimer

MAY 1954; NO. 207
Cover artist: Win Mortimer

OCTOBER 1951; NO. 176
Cover artist: Win Mortimer

SEPTEMBER 1953; NO. 199
Cover artist: Win Mortimer

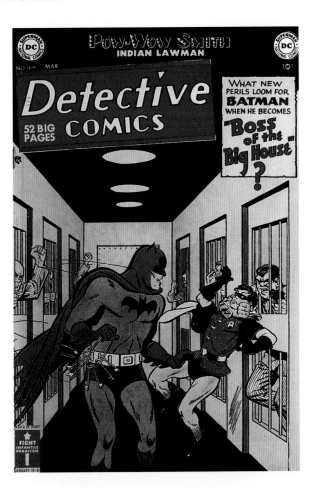

MARCH 1951; NO. 169
Cover artist: Win Mortimer

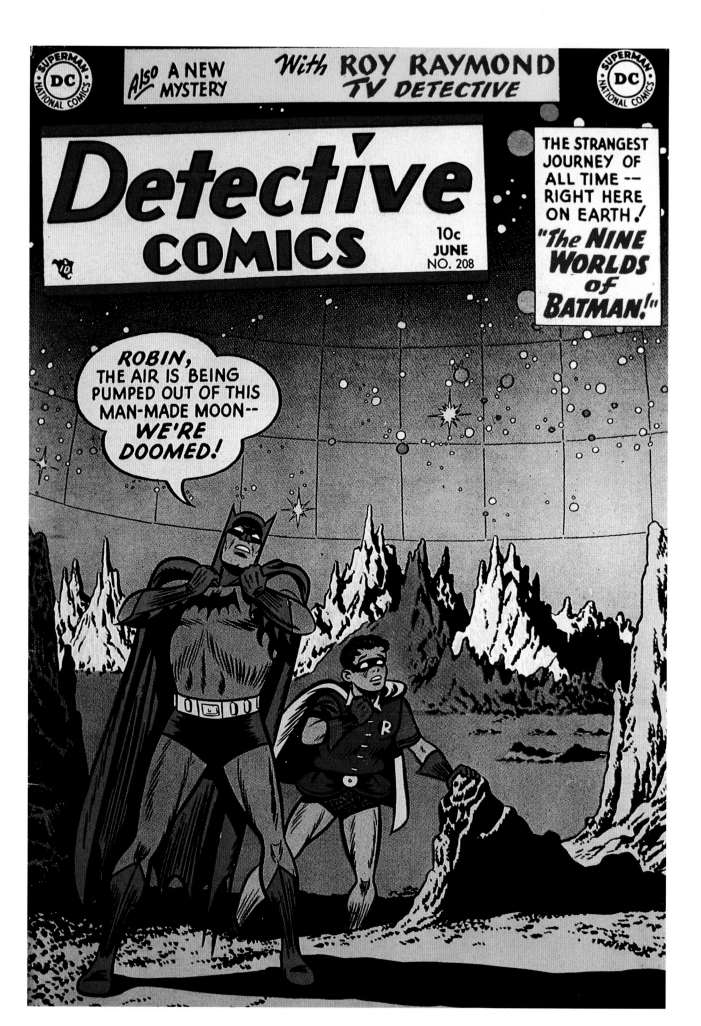

JUNE 1954; NO. 208
Cover artists: Curt Swan, Stan Kaye

Uncommon Occurrences

Batman and Robin typically limited their crime-fighting activities to Gotham City. Unlike Superman, who battled the Axis powers at home and abroad, Batman's World War II–era appearances only rarely made note of the war effort (covers 78, 101). This was due in part to Superman's incontrovertible superhuman abilities; Batman, after all, was not capable of quite the same heroics, like bending tank guns, ripping open submarines, or stopping exploding shells with his chest.

From time to time the writers placed the Dynamic Duo in some amazing situations that were sure to attract a reader's attention because they were so offbeat, such as battling the Frankenstein monster (cover 135). Other unusual scenarios saw Batman and Robin travel back in time (made possible by Professor Carter Nichols), enabling them to visit the banks of the Nile (cover 167) and to link up with Robin Hood (cover 116). And in one of the more bizarre twists, the Dynamic Duo even exchanged roles (cover 218).

APRIL 1946; NO. 110
Cover artist: Win Mortimer

NOVEMBER 1947; NO. 129
Cover artists: Jack Burnley, Charles Paris

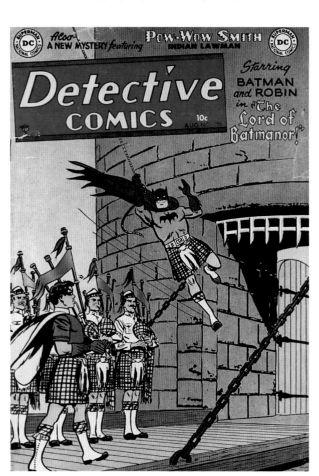

AUGUST 1953; NO. 198
Cover artist: Win Mortimer

OCTOBER 1946; NO. 116
Cover artist: Win Mortimer

APRIL 1943; NO. 74
Cover artist: Jerry Robinson

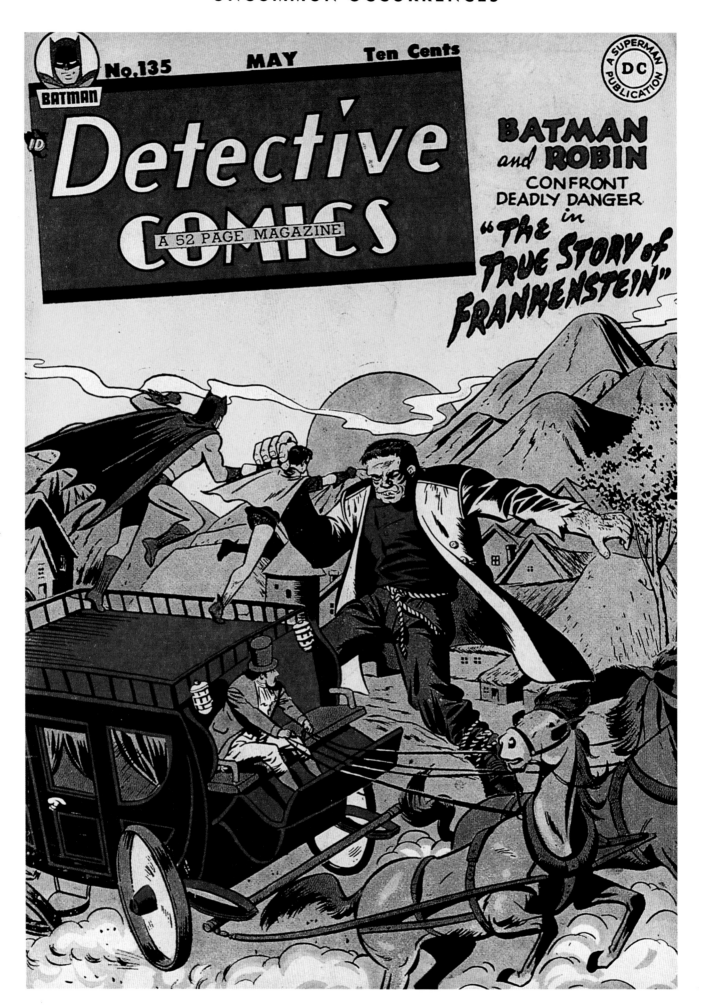

140

MAY 1948; NO. 135
Cover artists: Lew Sayre Schwartz, Bob Kane,
Win Mortimer, Charles Paris

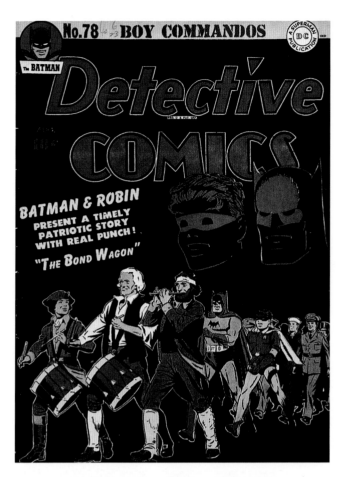

AUGUST 1943; NO. 78
Cover artists: Jack Burnley, George Roussos,
Jerry Robinson

DECEMBER 1945; NO. 106
Cover artist: Dick Sprang

DECEMBER 1954; NO. 214
Cover artist: Win Mortimer

DECEMBER 1951; NO. 178
Cover artist: Win Mortimer

APRIL 1955; NO. 218
Cover artist: Win Mortimer

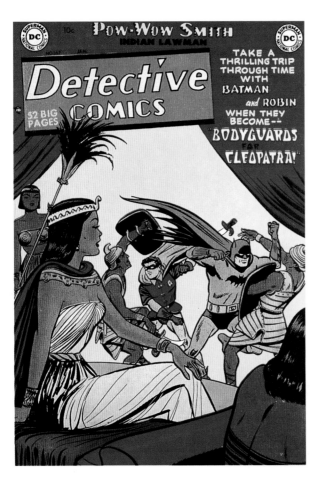

JANUARY 1951; NO. 167
Cover artist: Win Mortimer

JULY 1945; NO. 101
Cover artist: Dick Sprang

DECEMBER 1947; NO. 130
Cover artists: Bob Kane, Charles Paris

List of Artists

Numerals refer to page—not issue—numbers.